A CALL TO JOY

A CALL TO JOY

Living in the
Presence of God

MATTHEW KELLY

ISBN: 978-1-929266-00-5

A previous hardback edition of A CALL TO JOY was
published in 1997 by HarperSanFrancisco, a division of
HarperCollins Publishers.

First Beacon Publishing Edition published 1999.

Dynamic Catholic® and Be Bold. Be Catholic.®
and The Best Version of Yourself® are registered trademarks
of The Dynamic Catholic Institute.

Cover Design: Jim Warner
Photography: Stan Musilek

For more information on this title
and other books and CDs available through
the Dynamic Catholic Book Program, please visit:
www.DynamicCatholic.com

The Dynamic Catholic Institute
2200 Arbor Tech Drive
Hebron, KY 41048
Phone 1–859–980–7900
Email: info@DynamicCatholic.com

Printed in the United States of America.

TABLE OF CONTENTS

I would like to dedicate this book to my mother and father, who taught me how to love and how to be loved. If I can live what they have taught me, there is nothing more I need to know.

—〜〜—

Love Is Everything

A CALL TO JOY

n the midst of all the hustle and bustle of the world, there is a whisper in the marketplace. The whisper is the voice of God. He is calling to you. He is beckoning to you. He is gently inviting you to a quiet place, and His call is a *call to joy*.

If you listen, you can hear His voice saying, "Come to Me." He is calling you into His presence so that your life may become a dance for joy.

THE VOICE OF GOD

Joy is not simply a feeling of happiness. Joy is the all-intoxicating feeling of *becoming*. It is the greatest of emotional and spiritual sensations. We experience joy when we grow, and we grow when we live in the presence of God and listen to the promptings of the Holy Spirit. I have spent twenty-three years on this earth, and just four years ago I heard the *call to joy*.

———

As I was preparing for bed on the evening of April 7, 1993, I realized that I was at a crossroads in my life.

In some ways the day had been no different from any other. Early that morning, as my younger brothers rushed around preparing for school, I had gotten out of bed, wandered downstairs in my pajamas, taken a large glass from the cupboard, and filled it with orange juice. Then I'd sat down at our piano and had played and sung for some time. After my brothers had left for school and thus vacated the bathroom, I showered and went off to the university for the day.

Getting into bed that night, I reached for my Walkman from the bedside table so that I could listen to some music before I went to sleep. As I did, I sensed a strong external presence that was urging me not to pick up the Walkman. I ignored the sensation. When I put on the headphones, I had a similar feeling, only this time it was twice as powerful. Again I ignored it.

I turned my Walkman on, and after a few seconds of listening to the music, I felt the same urge for a third time. This time, however, it was almost overpowering. I knew it was something I had never experienced before. I took my Walkman off, got out of bed, and fell to my knees. As I knelt there in the darkness and silence, I asked myself why I was kneeling in the middle of my room at this hour. But before I could answer this question, I heard a voice speak to me—a voice as clear as any voice I have ever heard.

"Keep doing what you are doing. Believe in yourself and believe in Me," the voice said.

I looked around. There was no one else in the room. My brother was asleep and snoring in the room next to mine. I looked around again, but somehow I knew I wouldn't find anyone.

Thirteen words, yet because of them, my life would never be the same.

—〰—

Three days later I heard the voice for a second time. It was then that this mysterious person identified Himself as God the Father. From that moment on, these encounters with the Divine became a regular part of my day, and although they are now welcomed and appreciated, they have never lost their initial quality of being intriguingly unexpected. As those first days went by, God visited me three, four, five times a day—sometimes when I least anticipated it; sometimes for long periods and other times ever so briefly. He spoke to me as a friend, encouraging, guiding, counseling, and advising. He told me simple things and little by little began to open my eyes and ears to the spiritual realm. He constantly encouraged me to better myself, to strive heroically for holiness. He tried to inspire me to live every day with courage and fortitude. I continually failed Him, but He never stopped picking me up and giving me a fresh start, a new zeal. He taught me to spend time every day doing things that inspired me, from reading the Scriptures to watching young children at play.

To live an inspiring life, you must be inspired.

Since that first night, which remains engraved on my memory, I have had close to fifteen hundred similar visitations. Who is this Person who can be heard but not seen? I believe that the voice I hear is the voice of God. Throughout the ages, many have claimed to hear the voice of the Divine. Others have stood in judgment of those who have made such claims. Some people will accept no proof, while others judge by the fruits.

In those early days I too searched for some proof, other than the actual experience, that God was speaking to me. I didn't have to search far, for the fruit of the experience was a deep inner peace. As an initial proof, this was enough. Then as I began to apply what I heard to my daily life, this inner serenity grew stronger and deeper and my belief more and more firm. Recently in my travels, as I have witnessed people opening themselves to the message and applying it to their lives, I have seen that each of them has been touched in a different way. So it is finally in the hearts of these men and women from all walks of life and from many countries around the world that I have found the fruits of these messages—and thus the proof that they come from the Divine.

God speaks not only to me. He speaks to me so that I can hear, receive, understand, and share the message, but He also opens His mouth and whispers deep within the heart of every person who will humbly and sincerely listen.

If the message is true, then those who apply it to their lives will experience true freedom. The by-products of this freedom are peace, joy, and happiness. And these are the very things that we all desire.

In these pages I hope to unfold the message for you. I will try to reveal not only the person I am and the person I am not but also the person I wish to become. It is my hope that these pages will help you too to see the person you are, the person you are not, and the person you desire to be.

In this book I have tried to synthesize the wisdom that the voice of the Divine has shared with me over the past four years. It is practical wisdom for the journeying soul.

The journey of the soul is a difficult one. The same difficulties arise for all of us. For example, surely each of us in our own way has struggled with pride. Perhaps we have tried to stand up to this enemy and fight it on our own, but experience inevitably teaches us that pride will always win under such circumstances. Over time we come to see that victory over pride comes only with our humble surrender. The challenge is to develop ways of responding to such difficulties without surrendering our peace and joy.

The journey of the soul costs. It will cost you more than anything you have ever done in your life, but the rewards will prove everything else in your life to be insignificant in comparison. It is a journey or both the young and the old, the rich and the poor, for both men and women regardless of age, occupation, or vocation, and it is compatible with every honest human activity.

The journey is the struggle of the soul to seek, discover, and live truth.

As I began this journey, I found that the words of the Father inspired me, but so did many other things that I had not really noticed before. The daily struggles of people everywhere began to mean something to me. I was being pulled out of my self-centered world, and I was being shown a whole universe. The pieces of the puzzle of life slowly but noticeably began to fall into place.

The joy comes from the struggle.

My response was His request. My response was to struggle. I struggled to better myself in every area of my life. I struggled to remove the things from my life that I could now see were self-destructive and sinful. I saw that morality was not about right and wrong but about life and death, joy and misery. I struggled to live the wisdom that was being shared with me. I struggled then and I struggle now.

I have found that when I am struggling to better myself, to change, and to grow with courage and patience, my life becomes a dance. A dance for joy.

During the early days of my journey, my priorities began to change. I became less interested in parties and more interested in spending time one on one with my friends. Time spent alone became an indispensable part of my day, and I began to try to slow my life down.

Then one day, all of a sudden, it happened: the people around me, my family and friends, began to notice that I was changing. Some thought these changes were for the better, others were not so sure, but all of them wanted to know why.

In those early days I had found a confidant in a gentle, wise man, a priest who was about fifty years old. He seemed well versed in spiritual matters and had humility, charm, and the ability to apply the faith in practical ways to everyday life. I decided that I would share my experiences with few others, apart from him.

So when friends and family began to inquire about the changes that were taking place in my life, I tried to employ the gentleness of a dove and the subtlety of a serpent in my explanation. I told them that I was just beginning to appreciate truly all the wonderful people and things in my life because I now recognized that ultimately they were all gifts from God.

I was happy, but more important, I knew what was making me happy. The struggle brought me happiness.

Remember "the struggle" is the struggle to better yourself, to change, and to grow with courage and patience.

Many of my friends asked me, "Matthew, are you in love?" They looked disillusioned and disappointed when I told them that there was no new young lady in my life or in my heart. Activities I had previously spent endless amounts of time and energy pursuing became almost unimportant. I desired quiet time each day and I longed for people to understand and share the joy I was experiencing.

Then, after about three months of daily communication with the Divine, I began to share the story of my experiences with a dozen friends. These were all people who would try to understand and who would benefit from the message, I felt. If they thought I was crazy, they didn't say so; instead, their ongoing friendship shows me that they recognized and respected the profundity of what I told them.

I shared my joy with these people and experienced a whole new level of growth. These friends had come into my life at various stages, from as early as kindergarten to as recently as only weeks before my first encounter with the Divine. My experiences were beyond both their comprehension and mine, but together we tried to draw as much as we could from the messages. We struggled to discover our true selves, to become better people, to grow in virtue, and we encouraged one another in this struggle. It was an adventure—an adventure that I was happy to share with them and one that they were excited to share with me. An adventure that I now hope you too will join me in.

A DIFFERENT PATH

Life is meant to be a dance for joy. But instead of participating in this dance, most of us are struggling just to survive the pressures of each day. We occupy ourselves with smaller passions, such as cooking, reading, exercising, or gardening; we throw ourselves into watching sports such as baseball or motorcycle racing or playing football or golf. We allow these smaller passions to become our focus, but by doing so, we deny ourselves the experience of much greater realities. Though we pay a good deal of attention to maintaining our physical health by eating and exercising, we humans are actually a delicate composition of both matter and spirit, body and soul. In fact, what sets human beings above other animals is the soul, which is carefully linked with the will and the intellect. Yet the soul of humanity starves.

Perhaps the adventure on which I am inviting you is not the one that you have planned for your life. Perhaps this is a "different path" from the one you have had in mind. Perhaps what you read here will challenge the beliefs you currently hold.

I know the feeling. The voice challenged many beliefs I held. Up until the day when I began to hear the voice of God, I had been walking in a dark alley, though I was not aware of it. I didn't know that anything better than this dark alley existed. I didn't know that I could want more than that out of life. But in the moment when I began to hear God's voice, I was given an opportunity, an invitation, to take a "different path." A path that would take me on the only journey worth taking: the inner journey.

In man, Heaven and earth meet. Although the incredible advances of modern technology and medicine have led us to great discoveries in the material world, the spiritual realm remains enchanting uncharted territory. In every age a few brave souls have dared to venture into this realm. Their rewards invite us to take a closer look. It is this spiritual realm that is calling us forth today.

These supernatural realities came crashing into my world four short years ago when I was nineteen. In a quiet, unsuspecting moment, the barriers that separated Heaven from earth were torn down, and my eyes and ears were opened to the things of the spirit. Over the months and years, starting with that night, I have come to realize that the possibilities that exist for you and me are beyond our wildest imaginings. By placing our feet firmly on the ground and allowing our consciousness to be raised to Heaven, we can allow the wonders of the sacred to fill every moment of each day.

LOOKING BACK

When we look forward in our lives we see uncertainty. When we look back, the events of our lives fall together like the colored pieces in a kaleidoscope, forming a pattern with meaning. We are then able to see how certain

circumstances and events of the past have been part of an unfolding plan. By recognizing that a plan or pattern of providence has been at work in our past, we are able to move forward with trust despite the uncertainty that lies ahead.

Up until I heard the voice of God, my relationship with God was rather casual. I went to Mass on Sundays with my family, but I didn't understand. I prayed sometimes—when I wanted something. God was God and He was in Heaven, and I was Matthew and I was on earth.

———

A young boy of thirteen stands in the middle of a soccer field with his head hung, a tired and frustrated look on his face. His gold jersey with black trim carries the number nine and on his shoulders he carries the weight of the world—or at least the heavy responsibility of driving the little white ball into the back of the net. One goal would make all the difference.

At the other end of the field, the action of the game is found amid a group of young boys who look no different from the first to the eye of the stranger. The only noise to be heard is the shouting of coaches and the cheering of parents and peers from the sidelines. But there is someone screaming, crying out to be heard. It is a silent scream. In the middle of the field stands number nine, and in his heart he is calling out. He pleads, he begs, he prays, "Please God, if you let me score just one goal, I will . . . "

His prayer goes unheard by those on the sidelines, but it no doubt brings a smile to the face of God.

Looking back I can recall standing on the soccer field on numerous Saturday afternoons offering such a prayer of petition to God. I knew very little about God, but I believed that He could do anything. My prayers enjoyed varying degrees of success, and as a boy I couldn't figure out what exactly made a prayer successful.

Prayer is successful when you pray for what is good, true, honest, and just. Prayer is successful when you pray not to change God or another person but to change yourself. Prayer is successful when you pray for what God wants. Thy will be done . . .

There was another experience in my early years that seemed supernatural. Up until my last year of high school I played center forward on my school soccer team, and I considered my sole task to be scoring goals. I seemed to know as soon as I woke up on a Saturday morning whether our team would win or lose. I was seldom wrong, yet I was never able to explain this extra sense.

I recall one day getting into the car with my father to go to a game, and as he pulled out of the driveway he said to me, "Ready for a big win today?"

I paused, then replied, "Not today, Dad, not today." He warned me against the dangers of pessimism and gently encouraged me to adopt a more optimistic outlook. I assured him that I personally was intending to play my best game of the season but that I had a feeling the team wouldn't win that day.

Sometimes you know things. You do not know how you have come to know them, but deep within you there is an urge to listen to yourself, to trust yourself.

One of my greatest fascinations with soccer is the way in which a game can accelerate so quickly. But when I was playing, once I had the ball or was involved in the play, everything seemed to happen in slow motion. I felt I had as much time as I needed. The greatest feeling was to nail a ball into the back of the net with my head from a corner kick. I can still see the ball floating in slow motion across the mouth of the goal. I would move in on it from the edge of the penalty box, leap into the air, and move my head onto the ball. Goal!

My peers and my parents, my father in particular, would always express their awe at how quickly it all happened, but to me I had all day, as much time as I needed. It all happened in slow motion.

Before God began speaking to me, these experiences were the closest I came to the supernatural. And for me, at that point in my life, they were everything. On Saturday afternoons, playing soccer and scoring goals were my single focus; they became my greatest realities. I didn't know that anything greater existed. As I grew up, I allowed many different things to become my greatest realities: material possessions, money, pleasure, pain, problems, worries, successes, failures, joys, cricket, soccer, golf, girlfriends, schoolwork. I didn't yet know that these realities take on their true meaning, their true perspective, only when they are placed before the backdrop of eternity. For material possessions do not exist in eternity, nor does money, problems, worries, success, or failure.

**Only two things exist in eternity: joy and misery.
We have long labeled them Heaven and hell.
When you are with God, you dance for joy. This
we know as Heaven. When you are separated
from God, you are paralyzed by misery. This we
know as hell.**

It is only in these last few years that I have learned
how important it is to focus on supernatural realities
and to relate all the activities of my day to the supernatural realm. Slowly I have been taught to see the activities of my day in their true perspective before the
backdrop of eternity. I have been shown that what I become is more important than what I do.

Another aspect of my past that forms part of a meaningful pattern concerns the support and encouragement
I received from my parents. My mother and father possess a certain practical wisdom; in my life they have
told me few things but have shown me many. As I look
back at my developing understanding of God, I see that
in subtle ways my parents always gave me an underlying awareness of God, His goodness, and His importance in my life.

The only practice of prayer in which I ever participated at home was grace before meals. We sang it every
night before dinner. My father would elect one of us to
lead.

> The Lord is good to me, and so I thank the Lord for
> giving me the things I need, the sun, and the rain, and
> the apple seed; the Lord is good to me. Amen.

My seven brothers were gifted to varying degrees
with vocal ability—but I'm sure it always sounded
wonderful to God.

God was rarely spoken of in my home, but when He was, my parents made it clear that His presence in our lives was indispensable. I can recall times when my father would speak of a particular blessing. On each occasion he would finish by saying, "God has been good to this family."

He made his point. It was simple and it was clear. The oldest and the youngest of my brothers knew what Dad was saying, and it influenced me more than I realized.

In my childhood I only recall my parents telling me, or asking me, to pray once. When my youngest brother Hamish Phillip was born, I was eight years old. Hamish was born eleven weeks premature and with a clot on his brain. I don't remember the details of that day, but I do remember my father coming home that night. As we went to bed, he told us to ask God to take care of our new brother and our mother. It is the only time in my childhood that I can recall either of my parents asking me to pray. It was clear that God, and God alone, had the power to keep my newborn brother alive. The lesson was learned, not from a catechism but from life experience.

There was of course one other time when God was commonly spoken of in the house, and that was on Sunday morning. My brothers and I were never short of complaints.

"Dad, do we have to go to Mass?"

Once one of us had broken the ice, we would all voice our dissatisfaction. Needless to say, to young boys with no shortage of energy, Mass was at the most boring and at the least an unwelcome restraint. My father, however, displayed with unerring consistency his belief that the hour from ten to eleven every Sunday morning belonged to God.

As my teenage years came upon me, I, like all young people, was confronted by that all-encompassing, "What is right and what is wrong?" I seemed to have been gifted with a strong sense of what was right and what was wrong in different situations. Once again, through their treatment of my brothers and me, my parents had taught us the importance of fairness and justice.

Life is not fair, but we must endeavor to make it so.

Since I was ten, I can recall situations that were impossible for me to endure with silence and inaction. I can still feel one boy's fist in my stomach after I had tried to persuade him that he was committing an injustice by beating up a younger boy. As I grew older and my understanding of right and wrong developed, I was even more appalled at the injustices that were committed by teachers against students. Some teachers would punish one student for something but let others get away with the same offense. Other teachers would insult students in front of their peers. I felt the pain of those being victimized, and I saw life's bitter experiences destroying young men's ideals. They would comment, "There is no justice in the world." If they were right, it was only because there were no just people in *their* world.

In the few years that have passed since my childhood, these circumstances have not changed dramatically. In retrospect I can see that while our educators felt that they were just "putting us in touch with reality," they were in fact putting us in touch with their own bitter reality. Their behavior reflected their own broken dreams, and their example of compromise destroyed so many of my young friends' ideals. In school most of my friends learned to struggle just to survive and to grab what they could along the way. Such examples and leadership formed in my peers, and in most people of my generation, the mentality that you should get what you can when you can.

> **When you give to another, you fill yourself, and when you take selfishly, you empty yourself. Taking is not the same as receiving. When you graciously receive, you also fill yourself. Give and receive, but do not take.**

Fortunately some of my peers have discovered greater truths since high school. Some will discover as time goes by that there is more to life than this all-encompassing self-preservation and pampering. Sadly others will not.

By some grace and in accordance with a plan God held from the beginning, I never lost my deep conviction that to dream is the first step toward achieving anything. Growing up, I had heard it said that "if you shoot for the stars and fall short, you will still be on top of the world." I had a conviction that ideals were important for me and for society.

My first ideal was proposed by my father's actions, and these were pointed out to me and defined by my mother. When my mother chastised me for inappropriate behavior, she would always say, "Look at your father—there is a gentleman." To be a gentleman was the ideal. My father would say, "If you are a gentleman, you will go a long way in this world."

As time went by, this ideal was joined by those of peace, justice, love, and success. Only recently have my ideals been raised to an even higher level; now I realize that God asks only one thing of us, that He gives us just one ideal: sanctity, or holiness of life.

Holiness is about grasping the moments of each day and using them to grow and become a better person and about assisting others in achieving the same. It is this that gives glory to God.

Looking back I marvel at the people through whom God has spoken to me and the ways in which He has used them as His instruments in my development as a person and a son of God. In my childhood I didn't hear a voice, but I heard truth, and my heart was attracted to that truth. God is truth, and I am now able to recognize that whenever I have heard truth in my life, I have heard the voice of God. God speaks to us all. The voice of God is truth.

When you hear truth, you hear God.

SMILE, SAY LESS AND LISTEN MORE, PRAY, AND TRUST

Virtue is beautiful, profound, and immensely useful in ordinary everyday life. Virtue is practical.

In my early encounters with the Father, He began to instruct me about the inner life, the life of the spirit. I saw Him challenging me to be a better person. The words He spoke struck me deeply. Their simplicity yet profundity was utterly disarming. It was a testament to the fact that it is not only what is said but the love with which it is said that touches hearts. His gentleness tore down my personal biases while His warmth and firmness slowly began to erode my imperfections. The barriers I had built to block out His way were slowly dismantled, and I found myself submitting my whole being to the message.

There were of course some things that He said that had a greater effect on me than others. There is one short excerpt that lives with me every day. This line echoes in my head like music.

> *"Smile, say less and listen more, pray, and trust in Me, your Heavenly Father."*

This is one of the many things the Father has spoken that has had an ever-recurring and increasing effect on my life. It has been a constant struggle each day just to live this one sentence. This line alone expresses the most about how I wanted my life to change and how I continue to struggle to let it be so.

Smile

Oh, to smile! It is amazing the difference a smile can make. A smile can make your day, make your heart skip a beat, fill you with energy, bring you a little hope.

A smile is an invitation—an invitation to someone else to dance for joy.

But a fake smile is worse than no smile at all. I began to wonder how to smile more without forcing it to happen, without being fake. It was only a little while before I was led to see that it is like anything else—you cannot give what you do not have. I began to wonder what exactly a smile is. I came up with two things. A smile is an overflow and a connection. An overflow of joy and excitement for life that abides in a person's heart. And a connection with another person who shares our struggle. I was discovering that only one thing gave me that joy and excitement for life. Thanksgiving. By seeing the gifts in my life and taking time to ponder and appreciate them, I began to feel joy. I began to smile more. I smiled so much that as I said earlier, some of my friends thought I was in love, others thought I knew something they didn't—and both were right.

I was in love with life and its Author, and I had been given the rare jewel of knowing how to sustain that love. Smiling was only one of the streams that flowed from the spring of reflection and prayer.

The significance of smiling was reinforced during my first visit to America. My host was a kind, warmhearted gentleman who was a U.S. diplomat—a man of humor, intellect, and generosity. He had been affectionately named "Mr. Rob" by the first-grade class at the local school. As he drove me through the colorful autumn leaves of Connecticut, he recalled this story for me.

—⁓—

One day a priest found himself walking through the Bowery in New York City, a place where many homeless people can be found. The priest was with three friends, and all were on their way to take a ferry ride. As they walked along, they came upon a man dressed in rags and sitting on the pavement. He was very dirty and looked depressed. When he met the priest's eyes, he beckoned to him to come over. Touched, the priest moved toward him. But his friends quickly spoke up: "Come on, you don't want to go near that bum."

The priest ignored their warning and moved still closer while his friends watched in amazement. The priest said a few words to the man. Then he smiled and moved on to catch the ferry.

As they were waiting to board, the same man came running up to the priest, sobbing like a child; he pulled out a gun and said, "Father, just before you walked along this morning I was about to go down an alley and blow my brains out. When you came along I waved to you and you responded to my call, my cry, my plea. Then you spoke to me as you would speak to someone you loved, but it wasn't any of this that stopped me from doing what I had planned. As you started to leave, you looked deep into my eyes and smiled. It was the first sign of human affection that I have been shown in seven years, and I just wanted you to know that today your smile has given me life."

The two spoke for a while, and the priest discovered that this man had once been a doctor practicing at Johns Hopkins Hospital. Then the priest gave him his blessing and went on his way.

Later, the priest went to the hospital to find out what he could about this man. He brought the man's name up to various doctors and nurses and was told that he had in fact been a doctor there, but he was having some troubles so he left. No one knew where the priest could find him now.

Three years later the phone rang and the priest was greeted by a well-spoken voice saying, "Hello, I'm Dr. Lawson. Remember me? From the Bowery? I'm back at the hospital now. I just wanted you to know a smile can make a difference—sometimes all the difference."

If you do nothing else today, smile at someone who needs to see you smile.

Say Less and Listen More

"Say less and listen more." These five words have improved my relationships with people more than any others. When I reflected on these words, I came to realize that I didn't listen to people. I waited for them to finish speaking so I could start speaking. When I started listening to the people in my life, I discovered that each of them had a story.

Everyone has a story. Your story is the thread of your life. It is when we lose or forget our story that our lives begin to fall apart.

Without even being aware of it, people I would meet on planes or after my talks began to share with me the lessons and the wisdom of their lives. They shared the stories of their lives with me. I heard truth in their stories, I saw truth in their experiences. Through them and their lives, God was communicating these truths to me. I was learning from their experiences.

Experience is not the only teacher.

On one of my trips home to Australia from Ireland, I sat next to an Englishwoman and her daughter from London to Bangkok. They didn't seem very excited about traveling, and I wondered whether they were leaving loved ones behind. Our conversation led me to ask where they were going. They informed me they were going to Cambodia.

At the time Cambodia was experiencing a political and military revolt, so my curiosity and concern were heightened. The British government was advising no one go to Cambodia as there had already been British hostages taken.

I asked them how long they were planning to stay, and they seemed uncertain. The daughter then began to speak. She told me that three years ago her brother had gone to Cambodia and opened a restaurant with his girlfriend.

Since the trouble had started, he had kept in touch every five or six days and seemed confident that the area he was in would not be affected by the unrest.

"Three weeks ago we stopped hearing from him. We hope he is being held hostage. We fear worse. We are traveling with a British journalist to try to find him," she said.

In Bangkok we parted company after exchanging names and addresses, and I assured them of my prayers for their journey and their son and brother. Their uncertainty as to whether or not they would ever see him again made me so much more aware of the gift of my own family.

Two weeks later in Australia I was watching the evening news when a report came from Cambodia of an Australian girl and her British boyfriend who had opened a restaurant in Cambodia but who had been arrested during the unrest. For one month their whereabouts had not been known, but since political stability has been restored, a witness had confirmed that they had both been shot and killed trying to flee. When they announced the names, my heart sank. I didn't know where my companions from the plane were now, but they had lost a son and a brother and I felt their pain.

—ᴧᴧ—

The voice of God never ceases in our lives; He just uses different channels.

In more recent times during my travels I am constantly amazed at how God speaks to me through people. Whether it is a hotel attendant, someone sitting beside me on a train, an old man in a nursing home, or someone who speaks to me after one of my talks—they all share their stories with me, and in doing so they often answer questions I have been asking myself that very day. I have learned that God is wanting to give us the answers. When I was young my father used to tell me, "If you listen you will learn." He was right and I knew he was right way back then, yet I still struggle to live this truth. It is hard to listen to people, but when we do, the rewards are rich. So often we don't listen because we are too caught up in ourselves or too caught up in what we want to say.

We are always wanting to know more, yet we are often not prepared to listen. We want to know more, but we do not live what we already know.

The Greatest Change: To Pray and Trust

The change that has had the greatest effect on my life since I began to receive the messages is that I started to pray. I don't mean saying a couple of prayers before I go to bed or uttering a cry of petition when something isn't going the way I want it to. I mean really pray. I set time aside daily to communicate with God, to enter the supernatural realm and tap into the strength and wisdom of the ever-flowing waters of grace.

God the Father, the Father of all people, the Creator of everything, was visiting me in a way that was very real. It was extraordinary. The experience didn't belong entirely to this lifetime. He asked nothing of me except what I knew was ultimately for my own good. He did not ask me, much less tell me, to pray to Him. But He kept making one suggestion over and over again.

"Build a friendship with My Son Jesus."

This is what He said to me. He never told me to pray to Jesus. He merely suggested that Jesus had all the answers and that Jesus was my greatest friend.

Over time it became clear to me that the greatest act available to us is to be like God—to imitate Christ, the perfect man. I had always been taught that to aim for perfection in whatever I did was good and noble. Why shouldn't I aim to perfect my whole person?

My first attempts showed me that the task of achieving perfection was not as easy as I had supposed it would be, and by now I have well and truly learned that this task takes a lifetime of struggle.

The struggle takes place between the false self and the true self. The more we abandon the false self and surrender to the true self, the more we grow in perfection. This battle takes place primarily in our hearts. It is a battle between power and love, between the love of power and the power to love. As we discover and nurture our true selves through prayer and reflection, the power to love grows in our hearts and defeats its enemy, reducing our love of power.

I become discouraged now and then, but there always seems to be someone who offers encouragement just when I need it or a simple word from Holy Scripture that will keep me struggling along. And I still enjoy the voice of the Divine leading me, instructing me, and especially during these times encouraging me, saying:

"Try. This one word sums up all I ask of you . . . "

As I began to pray more and more, the days seemed to be filled with music and the dancing never ended. The mood of the music would change. There were some slow songs, and I had to learn a few new steps, but the music never stopped. In some ways it seemed like magic, but it wasn't. It was too real, too true, while magic is merely a fraud. Yet if it wasn't magic, it also wasn't natural. It was supernatural. I was dancing for joy. The sacred was moving me.

The greater the joy and the deeper the peace, the more I desired the solitude of prayer. There was something about the silence of the time I spent each day with Jesus. I would simply sit in His presence, close my eyes, and share with Him through a conversation of the mind the things that were worrying me, my plans for the day, the problems my family and friends were having, and the blessings that filled my life, for I was starting to recognize these more than ever before.

I began to spend three, four, five, six hours a day in prayer. I was neglecting my duties, and the voice of the Divine Father came to correct me. He encouraged me to seek Him more in every moment of the day by fulfilling my obligations and duties. Just as I have throughout my life with most of the activities I have been enthusiastic about, I had overdone it. I was being humbled once again, and I started over.

With so much changing on the inside, it was only a matter of time before something started to change on the outside. I was studying business at the University of Western Sydney and slowly my interest began to dwindle; what had only months earlier been a clear and mapped-out future began to lack certainty. Planning the future, moving toward a goal, having a purpose to fulfill had always been a big part of my life. Suddenly, I found myself not knowing exactly what I wanted the future to hold; even more important, I didn't know what God was going to hold out to me in the future.

I was unsure.

The difficulty was uncertainty. We are all faced with it at different times in our lives. It comes to us wearing different masks and can lead us either to fear, worry, frustration, and anxiety or to trusting surrender.

It was not long before it was revealed to me that I was being taught the next lesson in this Divine class. The lesson was trust. God the Father spoke to me about how a father has wonderful plans for his children. He promised me he had a wonderful plan for me and for all His children. He did not promise me a plan without pain. He hasn't broken His word on either count. It has been wonderful and, yes, so painful at times.

Day by day He revealed His plan. I was continually amazed. The problem was I wanted to be in control; I was used to being in control. He taught me that control and freedom are linked but not in the way so many of us think. By trying to control my future with plans, I thought I was gaining freedom, when really I was enslaving myself.

You will never be in control until you resolve not to be.

It is in surrendering that we find our freedom. The key to surrendering to the Divine plan is trust.

If we open our hearts to God's plans, He will lead us, but we must be patient and trusting.

———

In the depths of the forest there were three trees growing side by side, and one day they got to talking. One of the trees started the conversation, voicing his ambitions, saying: "When I get cut down I want to be a cradle to hold a baby, because cradles are the center of attention and affection for everybody within a household." With this the second tree spoke up in a loud voice: "When I get cut down I'd like to be a sailing yacht to carry rich and famous people to all the harbors of the world." A few moments passed and then finally the third tree spoke, saying quietly, "You know, if I am ever cut down I'd like to be a signpost to direct people along the right path. I would like to show people the way when they are lost and have gone astray."

Time went by and before long the three trees were cut down and taken off to the mill for processing. Soon a man came to the mill and took the first tree away. The first tree had expressed a desire to be a cradle. There was nothing wrong with that, but something else was planned. The man took the tree away and turned it into a dirty old stable to house sheep and cattle and donkeys.

Then another man came to the mill for the second tree. This tree wanted to be a sailing yacht and there was nothing wrong with that, but something else was planned. The second tree was turned into a filthy old fishing boat constantly filled with the rank smell of dead fish.

Before too long the third tree was also taken from the mill. The third tree wanted to be a signpost—truly a noble plan for a humble tree, but there was another plan. This third tree was taken away by a centurion and made into a cross for crucifying criminals.

Now it would seem that the plans and ambitions of the three trees had disappeared. It would seem that they had failed in all they had desired to achieve.

It was not long, however, before, on a cold winter's night, a young man and his wife came along. The wife was pregnant and they had nowhere to stay. So they decided to make that stable their home for the night. That mother was Mary and she gave birth to Jesus our Savior that night in the stable.

The stable, the first tree, wanted to be the center of attention and affection. It thought that to do this it had to be a cradle. It didn't. It needed to be a stable, because it was by becoming a stable that it became the center of attention and affection not only for the people of those times but for the people of all times. Even to this day that stable is still the focus of our attention and affection in our homes and churches at Christmas.

The Child grew up. He was the Christ, and He walked through the streets of the world proclaiming the Good News of the Kingdom of Heaven. The second tree, the fishing boat, got to carry the richest and most famous person ever to walk the face of the earth. The second tree had believed that to carry important people it would have to be a sailing yacht. The tree was wrong. It needed to be a fishing boat. As a fishing boat it became the platform from which our Savior delivered His message not only to the people of that time but to the people of all times.

But this man, Jesus, was just a young man, and He spoke His message far too clearly and uncompromisingly. Where there was darkness He was trying to shine a light, while other people were guarding the light switch. He challenged the people both above Him and below Him to change in a way that was far too direct for their liking. So as people always do when they don't like the message, they killed the messenger. They dragged Him outside the gates of the city, and on that cross, the third tree, they crucified Him.

The third tree wanted to be a signpost, and indeed it became the greatest signpost of all times. The cross is the signpost that leads us along the right path. The cross is the signpost that leads us back to the right path when we are lost and have gone astray.

Suffering puts us in touch with what is really important. Sacrifice spells out our commitment and confirms our love.

The three trees had plans and ambitions just as you and I do. But the trees could not have foreseen or planned what was actually in store for them. Neither can we. If only we would abandon ourselves to our Father's loving arms, but it is this prospect of abandoning ourselves to God that scares us so much. Rather than do so, we often abandon God and happiness at the same time.

It was by reflecting on my past that I began to develop trust. As I prayed, I recalled the way the pieces fit together in the kaleidoscope of my past; as I looked back, it was clear that there had been a "Planner." In this way, I learned to trust the Planner and realized that He was my Father and the Father of all of humanity. Our Father.

It quickly became apparent that my Heavenly Father had a plan for my happiness. In this plan my happiness and victory were assured. He called me to prayer so that He could open my eyes to the plan. As I slowly awakened to the realities of the spirit world, I began to see that nothing was a coincidence, that everything fit perfectly into a much greater plan than any of us could formulate in our own little minds. The plan was Divine.

Nothing in this life is a coincidence. There are no accidents, just providence. Providence, providence, all is providence.

Our happiness comes from seeking, finding, and struggling to live in harmony with this plan. The plan is truth, but it will never be imposed upon us.

No one can force you to be happy.

God has a plan for each of us, but He perfectly respects our personal freedom, our ability to choose for Him or against Him, our ability to choose life or death, our ability to choose happiness or unhappiness.

I know the plans I have for you, says the Lord, plans
for good and not evil, to give you a future and a hope.
Jeremiah 29:11

Clearly and absolutely, the only thing that matters at the end of the day is whether we have cooperated with this plan. Our individual correspondence with the plan develops inner harmony as well as world unity and peace. If we want to live in a peaceful world, we must first realize that we will never achieve this peace and harmony while the battles are still raging in our own hearts.

If it is in the plan that you will live, then you will have air to breathe.

To breathe is not a right; it is a gift.

One of the first steps toward being able to recognize and be in touch with the divine plan is discovering the difference between a right and a gift. In the modern Western world we have an interesting combination of an overdeveloped sense of rights and an overdeveloped ego. When the two are mixed together, they form an extremely harmful formula known as U^4 (unfulfilled, unhappy, unsatisfied, and unbearable).

Even a small dose of this in our lives prevents us from being able to see the plan. Worse still, it renders us blind to the miracles in our life. And failing to recognize the miracles in our lives is one of the major problems in our world.

What miracle occurred in your life today? The miracle of life, the miracle of friends, the miracle of laughter. I woke up this morning and the sun was shining on my face through the window. "It's good to be alive!" I said to myself.

I don't understand why I am alive, or why I wake up each day, how I breathe, and many other things, but I do know that one day I will not wake up. Death, however, is not a mystery. Life is the mystery. Life is sacred.

Life is to be reverenced in all its forms.

Life is a miracle. But like most people who have wandered through this world, I do not spend enough time pondering the sacredness, the mystery, the wonder, the gift of life. Whenever I *have* reflected on the mystery of life, my days have been greatly enriched.

Now I try to open myself to this life by trusting that I am where I am right now for a reason. There is a plan, a glorious plan—a plan full of miracles.

A Simple Message

"Smile, say less and listen more, pray, and trust in Me, your Heavenly Father." Such a simple message. It is simple yet profound. We talk about the need for things to change in this world. Smile three times more today than you did yesterday. Say three things less today than you did yesterday and listen to three more people. Pray for three minutes more today than you did yesterday. And trustingly surrender just three aspects of your life, great or small, to God who is your Father.

The world will begin to change when you begin to change.

GOD SPEAKS TO US TO ENCOURAGE US

Not everyone with his eyes closed is asleep, and not everyone with her eyes open can see. If you do not listen, you will never hear.

Throughout the ages God has been constantly in communication with humanity. In His wisdom He has used a variety of means to show man His ways. In the Scriptures we read over and over again of man's encounters with God. God said to Adam . . . God spoke to Moses, saying, . . . God said to Abraham. . . .

God speaks. Why are so many people, especially people of faith, so surprised to hear that God has communicated with someone? He spoke then and He speaks now. In my travels the question that has arisen so often and the question that has been a barrier that has stopped so many people from hearing the message is the question, Why? Why would God speak to Matthew Kelly—or to anyone?

I do not suppose that it is really for any of us to say why God would do anything, although we often take it upon ourselves to decide what we will and will not allow God to do or what is and what is not the work of God.

Let me tell you a story. When I was seven years old and in first grade, I remember week after week on Friday afternoons coming to the school gates and finding three or four of my brothers standing there very happy and excited because once again the school week was over and the weekend had come around. But week after week on Friday afternoons, I found myself coming to the school gates sad.

I recall one Friday afternoon in particular. The school bell rang and everyone rushed out of class and ran toward the gates. I gathered my things together slowly, packed my school bag, tidied my desk, and then dragged my school bag slowly toward the gate where I found four of my brothers; once again they were very happy and excited because the weekend had come around. But that Friday I was particularly sad, and I remember my mother coming to pick us up. Mum would park down at the end of the street and then walk up to get us.

We all walked to the car, and as we got close my mother took our school bags from us and put them in the back. Then I remember getting into the car—and bursting into tears. I had been holding the tears back all afternoon, and I couldn't hold them back any longer. My brothers looked at me, wondering what had happened, and when my mother saw me crying, she said, "What's wrong?"

I explained between sobs that on Friday afternoons in first grade we had our spelling test and that again I had failed. I always failed. I couldn't spell. I remember that day my mother took me home and held me in her arms, saying, "Everything is going to be all right. We will practice your spelling and you will get better."

Then she said to me, "How many did you get right in your spelling test today?" And I said, "Six—out of twenty." My mum said, "That's fine. If you get seven next week, on Friday afternoon I will take you straight from school and I will buy you a big bar of chocolate." I got seven, and I got my bar of chocolate. Then eight, and nine, and ten, and more chocolate. Twelve, fourteen, sixteen, and more chocolate. Eighteen, nineteen, twenty, and more chocolate. Until not only had I developed a love for chocolate but I could also spell.

I could spell—and that is why God speaks to us: to encourage us. And God is speaking to us all. Perhaps not in a distinct and audible voice but through the voices of the people in our lives on a daily basis, through those of the people who pass through our lives briefly, through the people who have lived as part of generations before us and whom we read about in books, through the circumstances and events of our lives, through the Scriptures, through the Church, and in hundreds of other ways, God is speaking. He is speaking to us to encourage us.

Because if you take a young boy who just got six right out of twenty on his spelling test and try to convince him that he can get twenty—impossible. But what is possible is to take that same young boy and convince him that with a little effort next week he can get seven, and then eight, and nine, and ten, and so on.

God speaks to us to encourage us.

God is speaking; the question is, are we listening? When we begin to take time out to listen patiently to the voice of God in our lives, we will see that He is speaking to us and that He is speaking to us to encourage us one by one, step by step, little by little.

My mother said to me, "Everything is going to be all right." She was right. What she said was true. In the truth of my mother's voice I heard God. For the voice of God is truth. In times of trouble and turmoil I listen to my mother's words again and trust that although I cannot see far ahead there is a plan for my good.

The clouds do not need to open and lightning to strike for God to speak. We need to develop the extra sense that allows us to hear God's voice in the gentle whispers of the afternoon breeze.

To hear His voice you must be willing to change and obey His words. To achieve the necessary frame of mind and heart, we must recognize that God is good and that He calls us to what is best. His challenge to change is much more than just that. His challenge to change is really a call to growth and to fulfillment. Fulfillment for a person is not a place, it is not a destination, it is a path. Journeying along the path is fulfilling. Standing still on the path is depressing.

When you stand still, you reject "the struggle" and you refuse to change and grow. Simultaneously you reject fulfillment, happiness, the dance for joy, and everything else that is eternally good.

Within each and every single one of us lies something of greater beauty than anything our eyes have ever rested on. Within each of us there is a flower wanting to bloom.

The flower within you that wants to bloom is your soul. The Divine Gardener wishes to work the ground. The Divine Gardener wishes to water the ground. He wishes to pull out the weeds and place the flower where it can get just the right amount of sunlight.

Listen to the voice of the Divine Gardener. Remember, when He points out your faults and failings, He is hoeing the earth of your soul and pulling out the weeds. Some parts of the gardening process are painful, but the pain gives birth to new life. Allow Him to direct you, to call you forth, to move you, remembering that He wants to place you where you will get just the right amount of sunlight.

Listen. Listen. Listen.

God is your Father. He is a loving Father with wonderful plans for His children. Regardless of

the greatest plan you can put together for yourself with the greatest power of your imagination,
His plan is better, greater, more exciting, and
more rewarding. Believe in His plan. Ask Him
to reveal His plan to you. Then listen. . . .

CHAPTER 2

WALKING WITH GOD

You will not be any happier today than you were yesterday unless you do something different, or at least in a different manner, with a different disposition or state of mind.

FOR decades now our Sunday gatherings at church have been growing smaller and smaller. Some people put it down to people's greater mobility and the increasing number of distractions on Sunday, such as sporting and other cultural events. No doubt these factors have contributed to the dwindling numbers, but don't they point to an even greater underlying problem?

Prayer, the sacraments, and indeed any spiritual exercise are all designed to assist and accelerate us along the path of salvation. The path of salvation is the path of fulfillment. Christ came to show us the way. We, like Christ, must ascend to the Father. Christianity is a process of rebirth and growth. To become Christianized is to become one with Christ.

For so long, Catholic men and women have believed that if they go to Mass on Sunday, then they are taking a step along the path of salvation; thus, they are one step closer to Heaven and can be considered good Christians. If they say the rosary, they take another step and can be considered very good Christians. If they go to Mass every day, they take seven steps along the path of salvation, instead of just one each week. The path of salvation is a path of change and growth. It is possible for people to go to Mass every week for fifty years and not be one step closer to salvation if they remain indifferent to the changes necessary for their fulfillment. What is more likely is that after attending Mass for all those years, these people will think, "I don't get anything out of Mass anymore," and they will stop attending.

This is the problem our Church currently faces. Men and women do not know how to participate, through the sacraments, in the life of the Church, through which we can receive the life-giving love of Christ.

Men and women around the world have been misled into creating an image of a God who has an endless list of rules and laws, a God who is constantly offended. But God didn't create the Sabbath for God; He created it for us. Prayer and the sacraments do not help God; they help us. Most people know that some actions are wrong; we refer to these as sins. Most people don't know why they are wrong. Is a sin a sin because it hurts God? Or is a sin a sin because it hurts us?

Contrary to popular belief, Catholicism is not a religion of sin and punishment, rules and regulations, but a religion of growth, fulfillment, love, and joy.

God is happy. In fact, God is Happiness. Our happiness is dependent on whether or not we actively take steps to unite ourselves with God. Sin separates us from God and makes us unhappy. When will we wake up and see that sin is self-destructive? Sin doesn't make God unhappy, it makes us unhappy. Our task is to become one with God. The attainment of everything good that we desire for ourselves, our neighbor, and our world is dependent on us becoming one with God. We become one with God by raising our hearts and minds to truth, goodness, and the things of the spirit. We become one with God through prayer and the sacraments.

It is through prayer, the sacraments, and indeed any spiritual activity that we learn to *walk with God*. When we walk with Him, we learn His ways, His wisdom, His love, and His boundless joy.

The path of salvation is an exciting journey; it is one designed for our own good, but often it is not portrayed or understood in this light.

WHAT HOLDS US BACK?

It doesn't matter how much money you spend on education; you cannot buy people the desire to learn. You must give it to them by having the desire yourself. And the desire to learn is born of the desire to grow and the courage to change.

If the proposed path is truly the way to the peace, joy, and happiness that each of us desires, why do so few walk this path?

One of the major obstacles is fear. We are scared of what we might lose. Even though deep within us we know that we stand to gain far more than we will have to give up, we have formed attachments to the very things that separate us from the happiness we desire. Because of these attachments and our tendency to search for the easiest way, we continue to walk the worldly path, enjoying the pleasures, enduring the suffering and emptiness, and foolishly believing that one day we will arrive at a set of material and pleasurable circumstances that will offer us completion and fulfillment.

Many people are constantly weighing in their minds how little of the divine path they can walk on this earth and still get into Heaven. In our minds we say to ourselves, "I want to go to Heaven, but I want to do this, *too*." We must consider God to be stupid; even worse, we do not begin to show signs of understanding Heaven. To go to Heaven one must reach his or her fulfillment and completion, which is the goal of this adventure, this journey that I am describing. To be one with God in Heaven, our fulfillment must be achieved, not partially but completely. If we do not complete the task in this life, then the necessary perfection and purification must take place in the next life before we enter Heaven.

You were created for something specific: not to *do* something but to *become* something. Jesus said, "Be perfect as your Heavenly Father is perfect." We are called to perfection. God's challenge in this call is for

each of us to do and become what it is He wants for us.
In this we find our fulfillment and are led to our com-
pletion. This completion is the perfection of a soul.
This perfection is necessary to enter Heaven.

God is perfect and God is Heaven. If something im-
perfect were to become a part of Heaven, Heaven would
no longer be Heaven. This perfection, however, cannot
be achieved with all the effort of a lifetime. It is not the
perfection of this world. It comes from a trusting surrender. God achieves the work of perfection within a
person—we must allow Him to do it.

Perfection is not an optional aspect of the journey of
the soul. It is essential. And like most things, if you put
it off, it only gets harder.

The world is full of empty promises. The world is
full of quick fixes and easy roads. None of these quick
fixes brings us the fulfillment and happiness that we
desire above all else. None of these easy roads leads to
Heaven.

—◠◡◠—

Once upon a time there was a young Native American
boy who was sent out into the wilderness for thirty
days as part of his initiation into his tribe. During this
time he was expected to take care of himself, to defend
himself, and find sufficient food to survive.

For several days everything went well, until he came
to an area where there didn't seem to be much of a food
supply. The young boy kept wandering and searching
for his fill, but as the days went by, there seemed to be
less and less food. Very hungry, he wandered up onto a
high mountain. As he walked up the mountain, a rattlesnake slithered into his path. The snake said to the boy,

"Young man, I am lost up here in the mountains and I cannot find my way down. I know you know the way. Will you please lead me down? Otherwise I am sure to die up here."

The boy replied, "I know what you are. You're a rattlesnake. You could kill me with just one bite."

The snake persisted, "Young man, you look very hungry."

"I have not eaten in many days," the boy replied.

"If you show me the way to the bottom of the mountain, I will show you where there is food. I will lead you to a banquet and then I will dance for you."

The boy was silent until the snake danced before him a little. The snake said, "Am I not beautiful when I dance?"

The boy said, "You are beautiful when you dance, but I know what you can do to me. You could bite and kill me."

"I promise that if you lead me down the mountain I will lead you to food and be of no harm to you," the snake said.

Desperate, the boy said, "You promise?"

And the snake repeated, "I do."

The young man led the snake down the mountain, and as promised, the snake led the boy to food. The snake laid such a banquet before the young man that he felt like a king. Then the snake began to dance for the boy and the boy began to dance with the snake. Faster than the boy could blink an eye, the snake turned on the boy, struck out, and bit him. He fell to the ground and cried. He cried and cried for the pain was great. Between tears and shouts of pain he said to the snake, "You promised! You promised you wouldn't bite me!"

The snake smiled and laughed and said, "You knew what I was when you picked me up."

The rattlesnake of the material world is always making promises that it cannot keep. Pleasure and possessions are always making promises that they cannot keep.

What is it in your life that sooner or later is going to turn on you and bite you?

———

Our desire to take the path of least resistance can also prevent us from walking the path of truth, happiness, and freedom. We don't want to rock the boat. We don't want our friends to think we are different. We don't want to upset anyone.

Are your friends as happy and fulfilled as you want to be?

You don't want your friends to think you are different, but you don't want to be like them. So you have to be different; otherwise you *will* end up like them. And if ending up like them means being caught up in the things of this world and forming disordered attachments, then you will end up unhappy.

If you want to experience a happiness and joy that are radically different from your present state, then you must adopt a radically different lifestyle.

What holds us back? More than anything else, we do. We hold ourselves back from the very things we desire. We hold ourselves back because we have little, if any, respect for ourselves. If we had respect for ourselves, we would take some time each day to evaluate what is best for us—not in a selfish sense but in terms of which decisions will lead us to be better people and thus attain the joy and fulfillment we were created for. Having ascertained what is best for us, we would realize that this goal is the truest and deepest desire of our hearts. Then we would struggle with all our hearts, minds, and strength to make this goal the focus of our lives. In doing so we would begin to love God with our whole hearts, minds, and strength.

Our lack of respect for ourselves is what holds us back.

OUR GREATEST FEAR

When you acknowledge your imperfections, you are on the brink of great growth and wonderful times.

None of us is perfect. This is a truth that most of us learn early in life. Yet though we are not perfect, we are perfectible.

We have all witnessed ourselves and others failing in different areas of our lives. Some allow their failure to be transformed into despair and defeat. Others are able to get up, move on, and struggle again.

Some failures just *look* like failures. Other failures really are failures and need to be recognized as such.

Vincent van Gogh, the Dutch painter, is now hailed as one of the greatest artists of all time. But he did not enjoy the same acclaim and success during his lifetime. He painted 1,700 paintings; during his lifetime he sold only one of them, for a mere eighty-five dollars. Almost one hundred years to the day after his death, one of his paintings was sold at action for forty million dollars. Some failures just *look* like failures.

Imagine if after painting five pictures and not being able to sell them, van Gogh had quit. Today we would not have *Sunflowers* and so many of his other works to enjoy.

———

There are hundreds of examples of men and women who have persisted despite failure or apparent failure. Another of these is Babe Ruth, one of the greatest baseball players of all time. Babe Ruth knew one thing: he could hit a baseball out of the park. He did what he knew, and he did it often—a total of 714 times. But Babe Ruth had his share of failures too. He had to walk back to the dugout 1,330 times after striking out in front of thousands of people. Imagine if after Babe Ruth had struck out one hundred times he had said to himself, "Well, one hundred times is enough times to make any mistake. I quit." And yet so often we quit long before we have even reached one hundred.

———

How do you respond to failure? When you fail, particularly in your struggle to become a better person, how do you respond?

It is interesting to look at the circumstances in which both Judas and Peter found themselves just prior

to Jesus' death and then to compare how they responded. Judas betrayed Jesus. Peter turned his back
on and denied Jesus. They both failed. They both fell.
The difference is not that one of them failed and one
of them succeeded. No. The difference is how they responded to failure.

Judas experienced discouragement as a result of his
betrayal. He allowed his discouragement to be transformed by pride into despair. His pride was his defeat.
Peter also experienced discouragement as a result of his
denial. He allowed his discouragement to be transformed by humility into hope. His humility was his
victory.

Get used to failing. We all fail sometimes. It is often
the key to success. It is a big part of human existence
and an inevitable part of the struggle. But if you persevere you will emerge victorious and fulfilled. So often
it is our fear of failing that prevents us from attempting
to change and from seeking the joy we desire.

YOU AND YOUR WORLD

It is easy to see the need for change in our world today.
Teenage suicide rates are higher than they have ever
been. Murder has long been a sad reality in Western
culture, but now children in their early teens are mur-
dering infants or their parents. Drugs, abortion, home-
lessness, loneliness, and hunger—the list goes on and
on. What lies on the doorstep for the history of humanity? Is there any hope for our world? We know the answer is change, but where should we start?

—⌇⌇—

There once was a successful businessman who owned a very large company. Business was not too good, however, and his company was in a lot of trouble. It looked like the company might go down, and his competitors were ready to pounce on his market share. But this man had a plan that he knew, without a doubt, would revive his company.

It was Saturday morning and he was preparing a speech to give at his company's annual staff dinner that evening. In his speech, he wanted to show them the first part of his plan. But more than that, he wanted to emphasize that if his plan was to be speedily and successfully implemented, it was dependent on the individual response of each one of his employees.

That morning while writing his speech, his wife had to go out shopping. Ten minutes after she left, he heard a knock on the study door. There stood his seven-year-old son, who complained, "Dad, I'm bored."

The father attempted to play a game with the boy and write the speech at the same time. This went on for nearly two hours until the father realized that unless he could find some other way to amuse his son, he was not going to finish his speech in time. So he picked up a magazine and flipped through the pages until he found a large, brightly colored map of the world. He tore the page out and ripped it into many pieces. Throwing the pieces all over the living room floor, the father said, "Son, if you can put the map of the world back together, I will give you a dollar."

The child rushed to the task, eager to earn some extra pocket money, while the father returned to his study believing that he had just bought himself two or maybe three hours to finish his speech; he knew that his seven-year-old son had no idea what the map of the world looked like. But within ten minutes, he heard another knock on the study door, and there stood his smiling son with the completed puzzle in his hands. Amazed, the father said to the child, "Son, how did you finish it so quickly?"

The child smiled larger than ever and said, "Well, Dad, I had no idea what the map of the world looked like, but there was a picture of a man on the back. I put a piece of paper down on the floor. Then on top of that piece of paper I put the picture of the man together. I put another piece of paper on top and turned them both over. I took the top piece of paper off and there was the world, complete and in order."

As the father stood there in awe, the boy continued, "Dad, I figured if I got the man right, the world would be right."

—⁓—

The world as we know it today has been formed by the influence and effect of individuals, men and women just like ourselves. Similarly, our words and actions will form the world of tomorrow. When you begin to affect what you can affect, then you begin to have an effect. This may all sound very simple—and that's because it is. If you want the world to change, you must do everything within your power to make those changes come about.

A wise man was once asked, "What do you think most needs to change in the world?" He replied, "I do." Most people do not consider themselves perfect, yet even though we recognize our need to change and grow, we often do not take a single step toward doing so.

We are held back by our fear of the unknown. We are scared of what we might become if we change. Absurd as it may sound, we are scared of the very thing for which we were created: our fulfillment. We are cautious about abandoning what we do and what we have (even if these are self-destructive) because we have found in these things some sense of security. Sadly, however, these are also what hold us prisoner to our limitations. Many of us are scared to dream for fear that we might be disappointed. It is like a young woman who prays and dreams every day for that special young man to come into her life; then when he finally does, she becomes hesitant and wary, sometimes to the point that this confuses him and he walks away. She has focused on the fact that one day he might leave. Sometimes we are too hesitant to let our dreams become realities. And what she has focused on comes true.

Do not be afraid of your dreams coming true. Allow them to emerge and become realities in your life.

To look to the future, to hope for good things, to dream, to have the kind of vision that pierces into the future and then uses the present to achieve what has been envisioned is essential. Joseph's vision was to remain faithful to his call to love and cherish Jesus and Mary. His dream was of family. This was the means for him to attain the holiness that was his fulfillment and that gave glory to God.

Only by envisioning what it is we want to achieve and then by the power of the Spirit of God that dwells within us are we able to achieve anything. When an astronaut first walked on the moon, he and the rest of the crew were not just flying around up there in the vague hope of accomplishing something. No. Their efforts were focused on a specific goal. They had a dream.

The things that we have, the things that we do, and who we are form an identity. People identify with us according to these things, and our identity determines the level of respect we receive from people. Often we think we must acquire or do certain things in order to maintain this identity and sustain this respect.

Change threatens this identity and respect, which are false and idolatrous when the things that form this identity and gain us respect are the very things that prevent us from walking with God. So many people are alienated from God by the things that they think give meaning to their lives but that in fact bring them nothing but emptiness, unhappiness, and only momentary pleasure.

You cannot both change and stay as you are.

What holds us back from changing are things that do not help but hinder, things that bring not life and happiness but death, self-destruction, and sadness. Very often these things are detrimental to both our physical and our spiritual health. In some cases God wants us to give these things up and replace them with much grander things. In other cases He wants us to be more moderate. But always we are being called to raise our sights to the things that are above, to envision our fulfillment.

The first positive step for the journey of the soul is to recognize that you are not completely fulfilled. And then you must acknowledge that you cannot become more fulfilled while you remain exactly as you are today. If you are not fulfilled and happy today and yet, tomorrow you do everything the same way you did today, do you actually believe that you will be any happier?

Perhaps what is holding you back is the fact that in the past you have tried to change and been unsuccessful. Often people see the need for change in their lives and make a particular resolution to accomplish it. Although they have the best intentions, these people often fail to achieve the desired change. Why? Because they are focusing on the negative.

For example, a young man may realize that some of his thoughts and actions offend God and are detrimental to his development. Clearly he must struggle to remove such thoughts and actions from his life. But he views this struggle always as a sacrifice, and throughout the day his attention is devoted mostly to the sacrifice he is making. Before long, he has lost the initial zeal that led to his resolution, and the body, grieving for its "loss," leads him to fall once again.

He wanted to change. He was sincere and honest. He approached this change in a noble way. Perhaps he even gets up from his fall with a stronger resolution than before—yet again he falls. And perhaps he gets up again, but before long he falls again. After a while when he falls he no longer gets up, saying to himself, "I've tried honestly and sincerely to change, and here I am back where I started. This must just be how I am." Often it is here that people stay; believing they are not capable of change, they give up.

At this point the person is likely to have a colder,

harder heart than he started with; he has probably grown considerably sadder and more bitter, and is feeling greatly disillusioned about God.

He focused on the negative and became what he focused on.

There is no change necessary for your fulfillment and perfection that you are not capable of achieving with the assistance of the Divine.

The answer to this problem is to replace the old activity with a new activity. A person experiencing a problem in the area of purity can respond in several ways. For example, if he is constantly glaring lustfully at women as they walk down the street, his response can be twofold. First, he can learn to admire the pavement instead of scanning everything as he walks down the street, thus limiting the input to his imagination. Then, with his imagination and attention now his slaves, he can use them to begin a conversation with Christ, and he can try to sustain this conversation always and everywhere, "praying constantly" throughout the day.

Thus, far from focusing on the negative and the "sacrifice" being made, he moves forward by replacing the activity being removed with one much more positive, beautiful, and fruitful to his development.

Focus on the good, the noble, the just. Focus on the positive and hope in God.

It is the replacement of one activity with another of greater meaning and value that makes attempts to change successful.

If then you have been raised with Christ, seek the
things that are above.
Colossians 3:1

What the world needs is a new generation of the people of God who are prepared to abandon the materialism of these modern times. Men and women who know the value of a soul in the context of now and eternity. Men and women who are able to raise their eyes from the things of this world to the greater things of the next world. People who allow Heaven and earth to meet each day in their prayer and in every activity of their lives.

Making resolutions is an important part of the journey of any struggling soul. Resolutions give our hopes, goals, dreams, and vision direction and practicality.

> **There are some basic guidelines for making resolutions. Make only a few resolutions, preferably one at a time. Write each resolution down. Resolve first to perform your duties and obligations. Examine yourself with regard to your resolution early in the morning and before you retire at night. Do what you resolve. P.S. And when you fail, do not quit. Trust in God, humble yourself, and renew your resolution.**

Your family, your church, your society, your country, and your world need people who are prepared to accept the responsibility of change.

I've often been asked by people after they have commented on the confused and troubled times we live in, "Do you think the world will ever change?" I reply, "The world is changing because whether we are aware of it or not, we are constantly changing. While you and I keep changing for the worse, the world will keep changing for the worse. When you and I start changing for the better, the world will begin to change for the better."

When Jesus Christ walked on this earth He had one message for every man and every woman He met. Whether it was the leper on the side of the road or the woman by the well, the Pharisees in the temple, the rich young man, or Nicodemus in the middle of the night, His message was the same. Jesus' message to these people was *"change."* Almost two thousands years have come and gone, but the message remains.

Jesus only spoke the words of the Father. Two thousand years ago God sent His only begotten Son, Jesus Christ, into the world to proclaim the message of change. The same Father sent the prophets with the same message. The same Father speaks to us today. His message is the same: change.

The truth of the Father is eternal and unchanging.

Change, take a risk, and you might end up happier than you ever thought possible.

THE KINGDOM OF GOD

The cry of every person's heart is a cry for happiness. More than ever people are searching in all the wrong places for the happiness they so desire. The most common mistake is to search for happiness in pleasure and material gain. This search is in vain; any happiness that comes from the pleasure of the flesh disappears as soon as the activity producing the pleasure ceases. Any happiness that comes as a result of material possessions vanishes if the material possession is removed.

The happiness that we should be concerned with as children of God is not the happiness of a healthy animal or the happiness of a person who has all he wants but a fulfillment deep within our hearts that pours forth peace, joy, and serenity. This happiness is not affected by the feelings and emotions that fluctuate through our bodies from one moment to the next. This happiness is not affected by the changing external circumstances of our lives. This happiness is a constant, the result of uniting our consciousness with the Spirit and every moment of our everyday lives with God. This is the only true happiness, and it is achieved through prayer.

Anything that is both true and good can only come from one source: God. He is the source of all truth and goodness. So the more we crave happiness, the more we are really craving God. Yet we tend to search in all the wrong places.

Didn't Jesus say, "The Kingdom of God is within you"? Surely in the Kingdom of God, of all kingdoms, there is happiness. But with our attention always focused on things external to us we have neglected to look within and find and drink from the pool of happiness that we have been seeking all the time.

Our yearning for happiness is therefore a call to spend time alone and in silence, to go within in order to discover ourselves and our God. The more we come to know God, the more we will be able to trust Him. The more we trust Him, the more we will be prepared to surrender our lives to Him. And the more we surrender our lives to Him, the happier we will be.

Pray, know, trust, surrender.

Our happiness is directly linked to how deeply we are able to discover the Kingdom of God. Our happiness is directly dependent on our personal relationship with Jesus. This is why it is so important for each of us to take time out of our busy schedules every day for prayer. If you want to be happy three days a week, pray three days a week. If you want a joy and a happiness that are consistent, you must pray consistently.

It is our attachment to the material world—and the complex of emotions that come with that attachment—that leads us to be anxious and unhappy. While at the same time our spirit is wanting to soar to great heights.

Within you there is a hidden potential to love. The Kingdom of God is the kingdom of love, and it is waiting to emerge within you. This love will begin to manifest in your life more and more when you take time to sit somewhere quietly, close your eyes, reflect on the love and example of Jesus Christ, and then try to imitate Him in every moment of your day.

THE WORLD IS A RIVER

Only a dead fish floats downstream.

Throughout my teenage years I never really enjoyed my study of science. Science did not come easily to me. I didn't understand many of the lessons and remembered even fewer. The one thing that I do recall from my science classes, however, is the theory of osmosis. My teacher would say over and over again, "What is more dense filters through to what is less dense."
Recently I have come to see that osmosis has a practical application in my everyday life and in that of the people around me. For we are all human beings, and as such we are social beings. We engage in the process of in-

teraction. We influence and we are influenced. And this process of influencing and being influenced is osmosis. Each day I go out into a world that is fast paced, busy, noisy, and opinionated. If I do not know what I want and where I want to go, then this world will swallow me up. It will be more dense and I will be less dense. What is more dense filters through to what is less dense.

Regardless of our religious beliefs, we all understand the need for personal density so that we do not get pushed around by the world. This density is developed by discovering more about our true selves. This discovery takes place in the silence of prayer.

—◦◦◦—

So often the problem in our lives lies not so much in the fact that we are not honest with others or that others are not honest with us but in the fact that we are not honest with ourselves.

Be honest with yourself; this is the first step in the dance. In fact, in the process of learning to dance for joy, being honest with yourself is like learning to walk.

We know that some things are right and that some things are wrong. Listen to yourself. When you feel that a certain action is wrong, do not think of it so much as being wrong but as being a violation of yourself. Actions that we understand as being wrong are wrong because they are ultimately self-destructive. Remove the words *right* and *wrong* from your moral vocabulary and replace them with an understanding of what is best for the development of all the people involved in any given situation.

Do not do something simply because it is right. Do it because as a body-soul composite it will lead to fulfillment.

Dare to know yourself. In coming to know ourselves we will be challenged to change. And these changes will strengthen our character; they will make us more "dense."

The density required to influence rather than be influenced is the result of thoughtful reflection and prayer. When we are influenced against our will, that influence is always negative. We must have an essential strength of character if our true self is to emerge, and this strength is intrinsically linked with grace. By making many common mistakes, I have come to see that when I take the time to reflect and pray in silence, then I have the density, or strength of character, to resist the pressures and influences of the world. I become more dense than my environment. And what is more dense filters through to what is less dense. This density enables me to influence society in a positive Christian way.

Strength of character comes from prayer.

Prayer enables us to get in touch with the deepest desires of our hearts. It allows us to go beyond our shallow and superficial desires and to discover what it is that we truly want.

As we begin to assess how we use our time and expend our energy, we will soon recognize the first and most basic truth, the underlying principle of the spiritual life: whatever you do to another you do to yourself. Life is a turbulent river. I am standing in the middle with water up to my chest, facing upstream. Each day I throw my thoughts, words, and actions upstream. Eventually, whatever I put out comes straight back down the river of life and hits me in the face. Ultimately, in this life, and certainly in the final analysis, you get what you give.

We break and separate. God heals and unites. We place God far away. God says to us, "I live in you and you live in me." We build fences between each other. God says to us, "You are all parts of the one body."

Most of humanity knows this principle as the Golden Rule: "In everything do to others as you would have them do to you" (Matthew 7:12).

One thing that the Father said that affected me tremendously was this: "Ask yourself at the end of each day, 'Whom did I treat the worst today?' That is how you have treated me."

For weeks after I received this message, the last thing I thought about before I went to sleep was how I had treated people that day and whom I had treated the worst. Such self-examination really helped me to see the hypocrisy and lovelessness of my ways. When I treat people with rudeness, impatience, or arrogance, I am treating God in the same way. And this is the same God before whom I then kneel in prayer.

I am a hypocrite. Does this mean that I should not pray, because I do not live the resolutions my prayer leads me to make? No. By ceasing to pray, I would abandon the one means of overcoming my hypocrisy. Spiritual laws are based on our needs—our real needs. If we were able always to operate based on the deepest desire of our hearts, we would not have to ask the question, "What is right and what is wrong?" We would simply ask the question, "Which action is best for me?"

If we can develop the ability to be in touch with the deepest desires of our hearts and foster the strength of character to follow these desires, then we will never break a spiritual law.

> **Until you are able to operate at the level of the deepest desires of your heart, spiritual laws will assist in achieving that state.**

The problem in breaking a spiritual law lies not so much in that we offend God by committing that act, but in that we violate ourselves.

When I treat people poorly by not giving them my attention in a conversation, I violate myself. By not giving them due attention, I harden my heart and build a barrier between my true self and the self that those around me know. I weigh my true self down and prevent my true self from emerging.

If I don't have time to listen to another person, what I am really saying is I don't have time to listen to myself. If I won't take time to listen to myself, I won't take time to listen to God, and before too long my real self will be forgotten and replaced by a false image. This image will be nothing but a composite of the defects and flaws life's experiences produce in an unguarded person. I will then have successfully and completely violated myself.

Someone wiser than me will see my unhappiness and recognize its source and will say to me, "You don't seem happy." No one likes to be accused of being unhappy, so I will refute his observations, knowing that neither he nor I will be convinced. I will say I am free. The truth is I am a prisoner.

Thus, the saddest part of this scenario is that when we avoid prayer and reflective silence, we never really discover the violations we are committing against ourselves.

The world is a raging river. Paradise lies upstream, but you must swim hard and strong to get there. There is no room for complacency or the type of contentment that is really laziness. You cannot stay still. You must either swim and move upstream, stand still, or swim downstream. Do nothing, stand still, and the waters will carry you out into the deep dark ocean where you will drown in the worries and anxieties of this life. Swim downstream, and this fate will be yours even sooner.

Swim upstream and you will experience the struggle and the pain, but your rewards will be fulfillment and unshakable joy.

CHAPTER 3

BUILDING BLOCKS OF THE SPIRITUAL LIFE

"God is love." When a man loves, he expresses himself with virtue. Virtue is truth, and truth begets love. The greatest act available to man is to be like God. When you love, you become like God.

How would you describe yourself? What kind of person are you? Are you the person you want to be? If you met a person today with patience, kindness, humility, gentleness, fortitude, generosity, and a deep sense of love, would you admire or despise that person? Would you place that person on a pedestal, or would you try to be more like that person?

When God speaks to me, He speaks about the person I am and the person I can be. He draws on images of the ideal and encourages me to allow those images to emerge from within me. He does not want me to be someone else. He does not want me to be something that I am not. God wants me to be the person I am truly. He calls this holiness, or sanctity. Being a saint is about allowing the real you to emerge from within. This can only be achieved if we are prepared to remove the junk that fills our hearts and buries our true self.

The compelling fact that shines through all God has told me is that truth is attractive. When you are true to yourself, you grow in holiness. When the truth shines in a person, no darkness can put that light out. This is the holiness to which, through the messages, God is calling me—and not only me but you and indeed every man and every woman. God calls us all to holiness, and holiness is synonymous with happiness.

Yet in this world of ours, holiness is commonly misunderstood. In fact, a series of unattractive images often comes to mind when the word *holiness* is mentioned.

Some of us associate the word *holiness* with the old lady who spends twelve hours a day in a dark church praying on her knees. Others believe that in order to be holy you must walk around with a halo on, and you must never smile or have any fun. These ideas and illusions make holiness out to be unnatural and unattractive.

There is nothing more attractive than holiness; this is the reality.

Some people do not want to let God into their lives because they think He will spoil the party. God is the life of the party.

Up until God intervened in my life in this profound way, the ideal that I tried to live by was one that my parents had set before me in my childhood. I was taught the importance of being a gentleman. I strove for this ideal, to be good-natured, polite, and thoughtful, someone who would rather help another than hurt another or see another suffer. I tried to allow this ideal to emerge in my actions, but as a child with seven brothers, there were many occasions when my unchanneled energy brought a reprimand from my parents or teachers.

The "voice" encouraged me to adopt a much higher ideal. I did. My actions now seek to uphold the holy ideal of sanctity. Holiness, I discovered, was accessible to me in every moment of the day. Holiness is not something that a person has got or can get; it is something a person seeks. To seek to be holy is to be holy. And so I sought it like everything else I have ever sought—with unrelenting energy.

THE PREREQUISITE

The one prerequisite for the journey is faith. Fortunately, this is something that no one is without. The question is not *do* we believe but *what* do we believe.

We all believe something. Some people believe there is no God. They will tell you of the big bang theory or some other scientific explanation for the beginning of life. I believe in God not because of any proof that anyone has ever given me but because deep within I feel a yearning, something tells me that there is a God and that He is the good Creator.

Perhaps there will always be those who believe that all that surrounds them is the result of a big bang caused by a chemical reaction. But I must ask, who created the chemicals? And of course these people will have some retort. Arguments for the existence of God are external and useless if people will not listen to the whispers of their own hearts.

If you blow up a library, what are the chances of all the letters from all the books falling together and forming a dictionary? There is much less chance that all the beauty, wonder, and complexity that surround you are the result of an unintelligent bang.

Faith is not born from an external proof but rather emerges from within a person. It is not something that we acquire at a certain point in our lives; it is rather something we have always had but are perhaps only now uncovering. Engraved on the heart of every person is the sense that there is a being who always was, always will be, and is the Creator; that this being is not capable of deceiving or being deceived; and that men and women were created to love this being. We call this being God.

Faith then is about trusting in God, seeking to know and understand His ways, and struggling to follow and live in His ways. This is the life of faith and the way to fulfillment.

In His loving providence, God sent to the world His Son Jesus Christ to show us we could live in God's ways.

The recorded miracles of Jesus support His divinity.

Throughout the ages there has been a desire in the hearts of men and women to be closer to their God.

This desire within our hearts reflects a desire within God. God's delight is to be with His people. There are of course many people throughout the history of humanity who have claimed to be divine. However, one stands out to the attentive soul. Born nearly two thousand years ago, this man claimed to be the Messiah that the Jews had long awaited. The Jewish Scriptures contained many prophecies about the coming Messiah. It is important to look at the nature of these prophecies. This man is not a character from a myth or legend. He is a documented figure in history. His name was Jesus.

The following is a historical description of Jesus by Publius Lentulus, governor of Judea, addressed to Tiberius Caesar, emperor of Rome. It was written in Aramaic on stone and found in an excavated city.

There lives, at this time, in Judea, a man of singular virtue whose name is Jesus Christ, whom the barbarians esteem as a prophet, but his followers love and adore him as the offspring of the immortal God. He calls back the dead from the graves, and heals all sorts of diseases with a word or a touch.

He is a tall man, and well shaped, of an amiable and reverend aspect; his hair of a color that can hardly be matched, the color of chestnut full ripe, falling in waves about his shoulders. His forehead high, large and imposing; his cheeks without spot or wrinkle, beautiful with lovely red; his nose and mouth formed with exquisite symmetry; his beard thick and of a color suitable to his hair, reaching below his chin. His eyes bright blue, clear and serene, look innocent, dignified, manly and mature. In proportion of his

body, most perfect and captivating, his hands and
arms most delectable to behold.

He rebukes with majesty, counsels with mildness,
his whole address, whether in word or in deed, being
eloquent and grave. No man has seen him laugh, yet
his manner is exceedingly pleasant; but he has wept
in the presence of men. He is temperate, modest and
wise; a man, for his extraordinary beauty and divine
perfections, surpassing the children of men in every
sense.

Few can claim to have been spoken of before their
birth and none like Jesus Christ. In Isaiah 11 it is prophesied that the Messiah would be born of the house of
David. Matthew 1:1 shows how this prophecy was fulfilled. In Genesis 49 it is prophesied that the Messiah
would be born of the tribe of Judah, one of the twelve
tribes of Israel. Matthew 1: fulfilled. In Micah 5 it is
prophesied that the Messiah would be born in Bethle-
hem. Matthew 2: fulfilled. In Isaiah 7 it is prophesied
that the Messiah would be born of a virgin mother.
Luke 1: fulfilled. Psalm 72 prophesied that kings would
come to adore the Messiah. Matthew 2: fulfilled. Psalm
41 prophesied that the Messiah would be betrayed.
Matthew 26: fulfilled. Zechariah 11 prophesied that the
Messiah would be sold for thirty pieces of silver.
Matthew 26: fulfilled. The nature of these prophecies
lead to the conclusion that only God could fulfill them.

Then there were the miracles of Jesus. A miracle is a
happening beyond the course of nature that has as an
explanation for its existence or occurrence the direct
intervention of God.

God is the author of all the physical laws of nature. It
is therefore within His power to alter the laws of nature.

It is also within His power to accelerate or slow down the course of natural occurrence. Therefore, a miracle is not miraculous to God; it is within His domain.

Throughout His life, Jesus Christ demonstrated that He was capable of the miraculous by His own power. These are used as testimony of His divinity. There are countless examples; let us look at only a few.

First, the fig tree: Walking along the road one day Jesus sees a fig tree. He approaches the fig tree only to find it barren. Finding it barren He curses it and it withers. Since God is the one who supports the life of plants, it is within His power to accelerate the decay.

Then there was the miracle of Cana where the water was changed into wine. God is the author of fermentation and therefore this miracle is within His power. If you can believe that Jesus is God, then you will have no difficulty believing that He performed such acts. If you are unable to believe in the divinity of Jesus, you will find it difficult to understand or believe His miracles even though they are documented historical facts.

Of all Jesus' miracles, the greatest and most comprehensively documented is His resurrection from the dead after three days in a tomb, as He had Himself prophesied. In the sacred Scriptures there are several recorded appearances after His resurrection. The three principal appearances are to the Apostles and are recorded in chapters 20 and 21 of John's gospel. In His first appearance Jesus says, "Peace be with you." In another of His appearances Jesus says, "Do you have any fish?" This is testimony of His bodily resurrection. He is not a ghost; ghosts do not eat. He has a body.

At some point in your life you are going to have to act in faith.

I cannot take you back to the time of Christ and allow you to witness firsthand His life and His miracles. At one point or another you are going to have to believe in something. I personally do not believe that proofs for God's existence lead someone to believe in God. Faith is something that springs from within a person. It is always there waiting to come forth, but a person must call it forth. There has never lived another man like Jesus of Nazareth.

The following poem captures something of the uniqueness of Jesus.

> He was born in a stable,
> In an obscure village,
> From there he traveled,
> Less than two hundred miles.
>
> He never won an election,
> He never went to college,
> He never owned a home,
> He never had a lot of money.
>
> He became a nomadic preacher,
> Popular opinion turned against him,
> He was betrayed by a close friend,
> And His other friends ran away.
>
> He was unjustly condemned to death,
> Crucified on a cross among common thieves,
> On a hill overlooking the town dump,
> And when dead, laid in a borrowed grave.
>
> Nineteen centuries have come and gone,
> Empires have risen and fallen,
> Mighty armies have marched,
> And powerful rulers have reigned.

Yet no one has affected men as much as He,
He is the central figure of the human race,
He is the Messiah, the Son of God,
JESUS CHRIST.

Author unknown

—◌◌◌—

A Polish man once told me of an experience he had as a
young boy in a small village in the mountains of Poland.
The Communists at the time were trying to discourage
those practicing religion. Part of their campaign was to
send "educated people," accompanied by the military,
into different villages; they would gather the people together—voluntarily, of course—and explain to them
why believing in God was foolish and naive.

They arrived one day in the Polish man's village and
began to call the people together for a gathering. Once
the people of the village were assembled, they began to
speak of God as something that had been invented only
by man.

The villagers were very simple people. Not a single
one of them had received any formal education beyond
the age of eleven or twelve. One of the speakers asked a
woman, "Do you believe in God?" She replied, "Yes,"
and with that the speakers and the military began to
laugh at her. The rest of the villagers stood silent and
stared at the Communist intruders with no emotion at
all on their faces.

Then the speaker said, "Why do you believe in God?
You cannot see God. Fools you are, uneducated fools."
They called for a lunch break and then proceeded to
offer the villagers all types of fine food and wine as part
of their attempt to win the people over to atheism.

When all the people had eaten well, the Communists called them together again and spoke for some time; then they invited the people of the village to ask any questions they might have.

There lived in the village a very wise old man. The people respected him a great deal and considered him an elder and a counselor to the community. He raised his hand to ask a question, and when he was acknowledged, he pointed to one of the speakers, the one who had said, "Why do you believe in God? You cannot see God," and asked, "Do you have a mother?" The man replied, "Of course I have a mother. Everyone has a mother."

The old man continued, "You expect us to believe that you have a mother even though we cannot see her. And yet you tell us not to believe in God because we cannot see Him. We cannot see your brain. Does that mean we should not believe that you have one?"

———

In faith we experience a little of Heaven on earth. In faith we can do things that the faithless call impossible. With faith in God, who is good and almighty, anything is possible.

LITTLE BY LITTLE

Our life of faith naturally breeds within us the virtue of patience. The energy and time of unbelievers are spent trying to get in control and stay in control of the emotional and material circumstances of their lives. Men and women of faith struggle rather to surrender to and trust in God and His providence. This surrender and trust free Christians of worry and anxiety and allow them to focus their energy on the realities of the present moment.

Patience is the ability to endure prevailing circumstances. Our practice of patience needs to extend to ourselves, our God, other people, and external situations. We should develop the ability to be patient with ourselves by not placing unreasonable expectations on ourselves and by being realistic about our abilities. Our patience should also be exercised in our relationship with God as we wait for Him to unfold His plan for us.

Perhaps the most difficult practice of patience involves other people. We all have our own way of doing things. Some people do things that just irritate us. Their actions seem irrational, or worse. In these situations our virtue is challenged. When we find ourselves irritated by other people and their ways, one way to soothe our irritation and transform it into understanding is to remember that we too at times irritate others by the way we do things.

Our patience is also tested when circumstances arise in our lives that are difficult, even painful, and that are out of our control. Children often cause such grief to their parents. Children act thoughtlessly, and their actions create a set of circumstances that cause parents much pain and anxiety. Is there a person in jail whose mother doesn't suffer? This is an extreme example, but in fact, children are always imprisoning themselves in one way or another. With them, as with all our loved ones, we most need to remember Saint Paul's words.

LOVE PATIENTLY

Saint Paul begins his famous words on love in 1 Corinthians 13 by saying, "Love is patient." Often it is those we love with whom we are most impatient. This is often due to the fact that we want to control those we love. We are called to love, and love is patient. We are called to love as God loves. His love endures, His love forbears, His love perseveres, and His love tolerates. His love is patient.

With those we love we should imitate the sun and God. We should love patiently and with allowance. Those we love will put clouds in the way of our rays of love. We should not try to move the clouds; we should just continue to shine and love.

When we lose our temper, we practice the opposite of patience. When things don't go as you have planned or wanted, take a few deep breaths, let a little time pass, and try to see the situation from five years down the road. No doubt you will recognize that it is really just a speck on the canvas of life. If you can learn in pressure-filled situations to adopt the position of a spectator from five years down the road, you will be more objective, you will make wiser decisions, and you will spare yourself the embarrassment of losing your temper and having to apologize later.

Often it is those little nagging situations that occur dozens of times a day that test our patience the most. But at other times in our lives the tides of life seem to turn against us and larger problems try to drag us down. A death in the family, a troubled relationship, a financial crisis, a miscarriage, the loss of a job—when any of these occurs, the tunnel of life can seem very dark. Time seems to pass slowly. One day can seem like a lifetime, and one night feels like a year. We look for light at the end of the tunnel but none appears. Sometimes just when we think things couldn't get any worse, a light appears at the end of the tunnel—but the only problem is, it's a train coming in the other direction. These are the times that test our faith and our patience. At such times we must remain focused on what it is we are trying to achieve in our lives. We must surrender to God and allow our patient sufferings to purify and perfect our souls. The only remedy I know for such times is to meditate on Heaven and the Crucifixion of Jesus. In many cases these meditations will not take away the pain and anguish, but they do help make sense of our sufferings. It is not possible to avoid all suffering in this lifetime. To try is the work of a fool and leads only to unhappiness and isolation.

Develop the virtue of patience. Be patient with yourself, your God, and your neighbor.

HUMILITY

The attainment of humility, or the struggle with pride, is one of those difficulties that arises for all of us along the path. Some of us encounter this struggle in a difficult time when we need the help of another but are too proud to admit our need.

If you will not admit your needs, they will never be met.

For others, recognizing that they have done something wrong, have made a mistake, is the challenge.

They are then faced with the need to apologize to someone, and this seems certain to dent their pride.

Wise people admit when they are wrong.

For other people, this struggle with pride comes wearing the mask of an uncertain future. In our pride we want to control. In our attainment of humility, we are prepared to surrender and trust.

Humility, or our lack of it, can greatly affect the way we relate to ourselves, our God, and other people. It also has an impact on our attitude toward our gifts and abilities. "What have you that you have not been given?" Paul reminds us.

Our lives are full of gifts, such as food, clothing, friends, and homes, to name only a few. Each of us has varying abilities to read and write, to sing and act, to laugh and make others laugh, to teach and to learn, to run and to swim, to play guitar or piano, to invent, to paint, to bear and raise children—the list is as long as there are people on this planet. We are all given many gifts and talents. The secret to success and happiness lies not merely in having these gifts and talents but in recognizing where they come from. God is the giver of gifts.

When we see the things, people, and abilities in our lives as gifts from God, we live humbly in the presence of the Lord and we dance for joy. There is no such thing as a self-made man. This concept is the height of human pride and arrogance. God makes men and women; He gives us abilities and talents. He gives us air to breathe and food to eat while we set about building our empires on this earth. Then, when we have built our empires, we seem to forget who created them, who gifted them, and who continues to sustain our lives.

Humility consists of recognizing two simple truths at the same time: first, our nothingness, imperfection, and sinfulness; and second, God's greatness and the great things He can do in and through us. We are instruments. A paintbrush doesn't take the praise for a masterpiece; the artist does.

Think of it like this: you and I are simply vessels. If by some chance the Divine Gardener has laid His hands on us and placed us in His garden, filled us with the richest of soils, and in those soils has planted many beautiful seeds, and if from one of the seeds has grown a beautiful tree from which come wonderful fruits while from the other seeds many pretty flowers put forth wonderful fragrances and splendid colors—what have you and I had to do with the fruit, the fragrance, or the color? Nothing. We are just the vessel. We are instruments in the hands of God. The question is, are we prepared to let God use us?

Surrendering your life to God is about making yourself available for Him. God works many wonders in the lives of those who make themselves available to Him.

There is no advance in the spiritual life without humility. As we enter deeper into relationship with God, we come to know ourselves better and better. This self-knowledge is often humiliating. But these humiliations give birth to the virtue of humility in a soul.

For example, for years you may have believed yourself to be a good Catholic because you went to Mass every Sunday, sent your children to Catholic schools, baked a cake every month for the bake sale, and cooked a meal occasionally for the parish priest. Then one day in the silence of a prayerful moment, the Lord shines a light into your soul. You come to see that in all those years you have not asked the Lord once what it is He wants you to do. In all those years, you have not once struggled to abandon a bad habit.

Prayer humbles us and opens our eyes to the person we really are and the person we can be.

When you come to a realization like this, you are at a crossroads in your life. To your left lies the road of pride. The road of pride is an easy one. There are no mountains to climb on this path; it is downhill all the way. It is a smooth path and gentle on your feet. But along it you will find no lasting happiness or fulfillment. These are found only in the high places. On your right lies the path to the high places. The high places are hard to reach. The road that leads to them you must pave for yourself with one after another self-revealing humiliation. This is the path of the humble and the way to Heaven.

THE SECRET

The greatest men and women in this world have an incredible ability to hide themselves humbly amid normality.

Amanda Wellings was nine years old and living in Princeton when both her parents and her teacher, Mrs. Bobak, were prepared to admit that she had a real problem with mathematics. The adults met to discuss the problem, and at first they decided that perhaps an hour of individual tutoring after school each day would help. Eight weeks and forty hours of tutoring later, they met again and reviewed Amanda's results. Nothing had changed. Amanda had failed her mathematics test every week.

At this point both the parents and the teacher agreed that mathematics was not one of Amanda's gifts and that they should encourage her to focus on her areas of giftedness.

Time passed and before too long Mrs. Bobak scheduled another meeting with Amanda's parents. As Tom and Susan Wellings walked into the office one evening, Susan immediately spoke up, "We are so glad you called us in to see you. We wanted to thank you for your work with Amanda, which has finally paid off."

Week after week Amanda's results had been improving in mathematics; she was now at the top of the class and had for the last three weeks not made a single mistake.

A confused Mrs. Bobak said, "But I called you here to congratulate you for *your* work with Amanda."

"We haven't done anything. It has been your after-school tutoring. We merely supervised her while she did her homework," Mr. Wellings said.

Mrs. Bobak replied, "But I have not tutored Amanda in nearly ten weeks—in fact, not since we last met. I told Amanda it was no longer necessary."

When Amanda's parents returned to their home, confused yet eager to know what had caused this remarkable change in their daughter's mathematics ability, Amanda was already asleep. So the next morning at the breakfast table Mr. Wellings looked at Mrs. Wellings and smiled, and then at Amanda and asked, "Amanda, darling, what has caused your grades to improve in mathematics, and where have you been after school when we thought you were with Mrs. Bobak?"

The little girl replied, "I heard about a man in town who was good with numbers. So the day Mrs. Bobak told me that she would not be tutoring me anymore, I stopped at his house. Tommy, the boy who sits next to me in school, had told me where he lived. I knocked on the door and explained my problem to the man. He was very nice and patient. He listened to me, and then when I finished he told me to come to visit at the same time every day after school. He said he would help me."

She continued, "Daddy, this man knows everything, even more than you. He taught me mathematics. It was the same stuff that Mrs. Bobak had tried to teach me, but it was different."

Amanda's mother interrupted her to ask, "What is the man's name?"

The young girl replied, "I'm not sure, because it has all sorts of letters and it's confusing. But it's something like Einstein."

Both parents just sat back and stared at each other. Amanda continued, "He told me that some of us are slower than others, but we all get there in the end."

—⁓—

Humility is the secret. It begins with admitting one very simple truth. Jesus said, "Without me you can do nothing" (John 15:5). But with Him and in Him "all things are possible." If in every moment of the day we can remind ourselves of these truths, our hearts will be ever more grateful, our works ever more effective, and our love ever purer.

FORTITUDE

As the days and weeks passed after my initial encounter with the Father, my journey of discovery began to pose another question in my life. I found that the more time I spent in the transforming solitude of silence, the more I desired this solitude. And as I began gradually to experience the fruits of facing myself, I desired the silence even more. It finally got to the point where I wanted to do nothing else but pursue this spiritual adventure.

My desire to study, do chores, and work was diminishing, and I began to neglect them all. As this occurred, my joy began to decrease. I spent more time and energy pursuing the adventure, but the joy decreased even more. I had lost the balance. Finally I began to realize that although I am a spiritual being, I live in the material world for a reason.

Very often it is the ordinary, the everyday, the material that connect us with the supernatural.

It was at this point that I was introduced to the ideas of fortitude and the principles of hard work. Fortitude was the tool that God offered me to combat the evils of laziness, procrastination, and disordered spiritual gluttony. Fortitude, I was told, is about doing what you have to do when you have to do it. It ensures constancy and firmness in the midst of difficulties.

I realized that we all possess these negative traits to varying degrees and that growing in fortitude is about mastering these bad habits. I reflected on the ways in which I was neglecting my duties, and I searched through the filing cabinets of my mind for people who seemed to be able to overcome these traits of laziness and procrastination. The person who came most to mind was one of my former teachers in school. Affectionately named "Uncle Pete," he was an inspiration back in high school and is still today. Whenever I need to adopt a "do it now" attitude to avoid procrastination and laziness, he always comes to mind.

As if it happened yesterday, I recall one occasion in my senior year of high school. I needed to discuss two small matters with him and collect a book from his office. I passed him in the corridor and said to him, "When would be a good time to get together to talk and to get that book from you?"

"Come on, let's do it now," he replied.

It was small. It was mundane. It was an everyday occurrence. And yet, because of it, I would never be the same. He, like so many others, had given me a gift of practical wisdom.

There was an attractiveness in how this man spoke and walked, about the way he treated people and the way he handled situations, particularly conflict situations. Even in high school, I had often sought a way to pinpoint what it was about him that I loved and admired so much. At that moment in the corridor, it was like a shaft of light made its way across my face.

Here was a man of fortitude. Fortitude is a virtue, and no virtue stands alone but is always supported by other virtues. He was wise enough to know that if you put something off, it will never get done. He taught me that if you take the time now to do what you need to do, it will save you time later. Peter Wade always did what he needed to do when he needed to do it.

If there was one reason why this man and I had crossed paths, it must have been so that I could learn this lesson. His every action displayed a passion for life and a passion for his work. He taught me the importance of this passion, and he gave me this passion like an unlit candle being touched to a flame. He taught me to have a passion for whatever I do. It didn't matter to him, it seemed, what his students did as long as they had a passion for it, worked hard, and paid attention to the details. I wonder if he knew the influence he was having on me and my friends during those four years when he faithfully served us. The world needs more teachers like him. He taught me fortitude not with a lecture or a textbook, not by telling me how to live my life, but by living his own life. He taught me fortitude before I even knew what the word meant. I will spend the rest of my life struggling to live fortitude in the way that he taught me. Laziness and procrastination are lies. Hard work and fortitude are truth.

LOVE

Every lesson in the spiritual life is a lesson in love. John tells us, "God is love."

> **When we try to develop our understanding of how God loves and to apply what we discover to our day-to-day living, our lives become awe inspiring.**

For so long and by so many, love has been misunderstood as an emotion generally aroused by an attractive element in a person or object outside ourselves. But love doesn't have to be based on an attraction.

Love is, rather, an attitude that God has toward Himself and toward creation. It is not an attitude that God has toward part of Himself and part of creation. God's love is universal.

The love we are called to in Christ is universal love. The love of a Christian is an attitude that one has toward God, self, and the rest of creation. Christian love is not an attitude that one has toward part of God, part of oneself, and part of creation.

For a person to be rude, mean, and impatient to people in general in his or her life but then to claim to love one person in particular is a contradiction; true love is universal.

It is toward this universal love that Christ leads us by His example and teachings. To love like God in this universal way is the struggle of every saint. It is the struggle to respect and love self, God, others, and nature.

The voice of the Father calls us all along the ways of truth and love.

Love is truth lived.

As I hear the voice of the Father, I gradually and painfully struggle to expand the truth in my life. I find that the more I live the truth I know, the more I am able to give to others selflessly. In this way, life becomes an exciting adventure.

JOY OR MISERY

Truth and joy are proportionally linked in our lives. The more we live truth, the more we experience joy. It cannot be put any other way. If you do what you know to be good and true, you will experience joy beyond compare. If you ignore the voice within you that is calling you to the ways of truth and love, you will be miserable and you will spread that misery.

As we live the truth, so shall we love and be loved. Truth lived increases our ability to love and our ability to be loved.

Holiness, I have learned, is about living the truth. Patience, kindness, humility, gentleness, and fortitude are all truths. And where there is truth, there is goodness, peace, joy, and love.

There is another world that exists beyond the senses. It is the world of the Divine, the realm of pure spirits. It is there that the angels dwell along with the generations past. Those who have served truth with their lives dwell with God. They live in God. Those who have been slaves to lies during their lifetime wish to forget that God exists, but they cannot for in every moment His existence is unforgettable. This is the afterlife. In this realm only two things exist—joy and misery.

Joy is the result of truth lived. Misery is the result of lies lived. Truth gives birth to joy, and lies give birth to misery in this life and the next.

It is in the afterlife that we will fully experience the fruits of our struggle to grow. In this life we experience only passing shadows of realities that exist in the supernatural realm. The experiences of joy and happiness that we have in this life are only dim reflections of the much greater realities that await us. Because we cannot yet experience these realities, we sometimes believe they do not exist. So we go on believing that the shadows are real things when they are only shadows. This is like believing that the shadow of a tree reflecting on a still lake is a tree. Admittedly it is beautiful, but you cannot eat the fruit of a shadow.

If you gave a baby a choice either to stay within the womb of its mother or to be born into this unknown world, the baby would choose to stay in the womb because there the child is safe and comfortable. But you and I know that this would be an absurd choice, not only because of the physical impossibility but because of how wonderful our opportunities are on this earth.

Perhaps the journey I am describing in the pages of this book is challenging you to leave the comfortable place in which you have been living. You know that from deep within, you are being called forth to something much greater, but you feel unsure because you cannot see, touch, hear, smell, or taste what is being offered to you. It all exists beyond the world of the senses. One day you will have no choice but to enter into this realm beyond sensation. Death will take us all there, just as a baby by nature is born at the appropriate time.

Nicodemus came to Jesus in the middle of the night. He asked Jesus how one was to enter the Kingdom, and Jesus told him that unless a man is born again he cannot enter the Kingdom of Heaven. Nicodemus did not understand, but his sincerity in his search for truth came through in his questioning. He asked the Master how it was possible for him at his age to go back into his mother's womb and be born again. And Jesus explained that Nicodemus must be born of the Spirit. Jesus was trying to expand Nicodemus's mind to take in the spiritual realm, just as He tries to do so for you and me today.

**Just because you do not understand something
does not mean that it is wrong.**

So many of the ancient peoples placed God far away
from themselves. They believed that by living in this
world and abiding by the law, they would be rewarded
in the next life with a place in the presence of God.
They drew clear and distinct barriers between the
physical realm and the spiritual realm. Jesus tried to get
them to see by His presence and by His actions to redeem and heal humanity that a man is a temple. The
temple image was very clear to the ancient people.
They understood the temple as the dwelling place of
God. They were not able to see and understand what
Jesus was saying because they had been blinded; their
practice of religion was concerned with obeying laws
and fulfilling obligations.

To walk the path of truth and love is difficult. It involves a great deal of renunciation of the self to allow
the Divine to emerge within. This is sometimes painful.

Joy is not the absence of pain.

The way of truth is a lifestyle. It is not a part-time occupation or hobby. It is not just one aspect of your
life—it *is* your life. It is a way of approaching each circumstance that this life puts before you. Those who
have lived such a life of holiness have told us that the
only way to understand the true value of things in this
life is to place them against the backdrop of eternity. It
is then that we are able to see things in their proper perspective.

If this were the only life and you did not possess an
immortal soul, I would encourage you to seek pleasure
and avoid pain. This, however, is not the only life, and

you do possess an immortal soul as well as your sensory body, so I encourage you to use your mind, your will, and your intellect to allow your soul to be the master of your body. Train your body to be directed by the soul. For the soul is eternal, and that which is eternal should lead that which is temporal.

This process has a cost, and yes, it is painful. You will have to pass up some of the pleasures of this world, but never forget, it is for your own good.

Every thought, word, and action in this life has eternal consequences.

Life passes us by so quickly. Think of it like this: let's assume that you will live for seventy-five years. Now suppose that you have just the next five minutes in which to decide what you want to do for the rest of your life. Your life, compared to eternity, is like those five minutes, and in this life, you must decide what you want to do for eternity. Five minutes compared to seventy-five years is almost insignificant. Seventy-five years compared to eternity holds even less significance.

There is another world, and all of us one day will find ourselves in it. The decisions and actions of our lives will determine where we take up lodging in the next world. There is joy and there is misery. No one can force either upon you. It is the exercise of your free will that will determine which you experience now and in eternity. The very foundation of this life is prayer and growth in virtue. It is only by embracing these that our true selves emerge.

CHAPTER 4

PRAYER

No vase can overflow if you never fill it up.

W HAT is prayer? Perhaps most of us can give the answer, in parrotlike fashion, "Prayer is raising one's heart and mind to God." But what does this mean to us practically? My travels in various parts of the world have shown me that while thousands of people can define prayer, very few know of its practical application to their lives.

In this chapter I would like to share with you the teaching of the Father regarding prayer, the ways I have found effective in applying prayer to my life, and the practical consequences of doing so.

If we are to know more deeply what prayer is, then we should try to understand simply and yet as completely as possible what we are trying to achieve through prayer. Put as simply as possible, in prayer we become one with God. Through prayer we become god-like; our imperfections are decreased, and His perfection within us is increased. When we lift our minds and hearts to God, we do so to become one with God.

This is a glorious image, but it will remain just that unless we seek to understand how such an image can be practically applied to our lives.

From a young age, millions of Christians have been taught that we are to adore God and that prayer is one way to fulfill that duty. We gain a valuable insight if we look at the prayerful function of adoration. For in one way prayer *is* about adoring God. But *how* do we do this? Do we fall helplessly at the feet of God and adore Him, begging His intercession, while otherwise we do nothing but sit around and feel sorry for ourselves? No. Should we adore God in the way that He wants to be adored *or* in the way that we want to adore Him?

When Jesus walked the face of this earth, He did not ask people to fall down before Him in awe, to place Him on a pedestal, or to make a king or political leader of Him. In fact, He discouraged all of these responses. In the gospels we read that every time people tried to place Him on a throne and appoint Him as a great leader or ruler, He quietly moved on to the next place, although His heart no doubt ached because another city had failed to understand the message He was trying to convey. Jesus didn't want people to feel useless before Him; He wanted them to realize their true potential in Him. Yes, His divinity demands adoration, but Jesus

wanted the greatest form of adoration. Jesus wanted
the greatest form of worship. Jesus wanted the people
to worship Him by imitating Him. Times have changed,
but God remains eternally the same. Today Jesus wants
the same perfect adoration as He did when He walked
the earth—imitation.

The greatest form of worship is imitation.

Imagine how it feels for a famous musician to play to
a packed stadium of one hundred thousand people and
to hear them all singing the words of his greatest hit.
Imagine how it feels to be a part of that crowd. Exhila-
rating. That is what Jesus wants to hear. He wants the
lives of those who love Him to be one profound love
song being sung in harmony as a testament to His own
love for humanity and as a witness to the unbelieving
world.

God wants us to be like Him. What are you capable
of? Do you want to be great? What is the greatest thing
you can do? The greatest act available to you is to be
like God. In prayer we come to know the ways of God.
When these ways become a part of a person's life, we
call them virtues. God places these virtues in our hearts
through meditation and reflection; once there, they will
emerge throughout the day in our words, thoughts, and
actions.

What is prayer? It is the process that leads men and
women to become more like God.

If we are to become more like God, this, of course,
presupposes changes. As we come to prayer, we must
approach God with an openness to change. As long as
we are not prepared to change, prayer will achieve
nothing in our lives, and we will be ruled by selfish

passions and live in anxious unhappiness. Any joy in our lives will be short lived.

Since prayer is about becoming more like God, the first step must be to get to know the God we are going to imitate. As our model we have been given Jesus, who is both true God and true man. We come to know God in different ways through prayer, but before we explore these, let us look briefly at what takes place in the hearts of men and women when they actively participate in prayer.

In prayer we come face to face with ourselves, with all our imperfections, faults, and failings. We do not, however, come to see these all at once. They are shown to us gradually. It is like the sunlight shining through the cracks in a stone wall. When we see our faults, we are really catching a glimpse of God—not in our faults, of course, but in the light that allows us to see our darkness.

Prayer is about uncovering and discovering truths—small truths and large truths, truths about ourselves and truths about our God. Life is about allowing the truths we discover about our God to emerge within us and become truths about ourselves.

The primary way in which we come to know God and His ways as Christians is through the Scriptures. Specifically the gospels are the revelation of Christ's life to all people. They tell us what He did and what He said, and they inspire us to act and speak in the same ways. Ignorance of the gospels is ignorance of Christ, as you cannot imitate someone you do not know.

Through the gospels we are fed. In thousands of ways we catch glimpses of God, and these at the same time reveal our faults and flaws. The gospels are thus always new and exciting. They probe the hearts of every man and woman and call us to the struggle to better ourselves.

—⁓—

Once upon a time there was a prince. The prince was a fine young man, caring in every way, but because he had a hunchback, it was difficult for him to look up. He spent most of his time looking at the ground.

One day the people of the area decided to build a statue in honor of the prince. The statue, however, stood straight and tall with no hunchback.

Every day the prince would walk to the center of town and would stand there for a short time looking at the statue. As time passed, the people began to notice that the hunch in the prince's back was not so bad— until finally one day the prince stood straight and tall with no hunchback at all.

Read the life of Christ. . . . Meditate on the different passages. . . . Imagine yourself present in the different scenes. . . . Rediscover the gospels.

Prayer brings to our lives focus and direction and protects us from disordered attachments. Prayer confirms our hearts, minds, wills, and intellects in what we really want. One of the greatest problems in the world is that people do not really know what they want. As a result they end up going with the flow; they become tools for other people's selfish desires and plans, which stem from greed and the desire for power. Evil gives birth to evil and makes slaves of humanity. Prayer allows us to clarify why we are here on this earth and reminds us that there is more to our lives than the time we spend here. Prayer puts us in touch with eternal realities.

THE AGELESS CALL

Since the beginning of time, God has beckoned humanity to participate in a relationship with Him. His ageless call is the call to prayer.

Adam had an intimate friendship with God. They walked together in the garden in the afternoon breeze. This relationship was Adam's prayer. God calls each of us to this friendship to discover and learn His ways of truth, goodness, love, serenity, and happiness.

It is true that we have nothing to give that could add to God. But by not praying we receive nothing from God's infinite greatness. God gains nothing from our prayer. We, and we alone, gain from prayer.

God is not an egotistical God. He doesn't call us to prayer in order to gratify His own ego. He doesn't call us to prayer to give us an opportunity to repay Him in some way for our lives. God doesn't call us to prayer to place a burden on our shoulders but to lift that burden from us. His mere essence is to give, and this He does through prayer. In giving to us, He challenges us simultaneously to renounce our selfish ways and to give to others.

One of the surest roads to happiness in this life is selflessness.

Why does God call humanity to prayer? Humanity universally desires peace, joy, love, and happiness. We experience these when we become one with God. Peace, joy, love, and happiness are the fruits of prayer.

Yet if this is true, if all men and women have universal desires for peace, joy, love, and happiness and if these things truly come to us from God through prayer, then why don't we pray? And if we desire peace, joy, love, and happiness to be consistent in our lives, then why don't we pray every day?

It is not uncommon these days to come across people who do not practice any form of public worship or prayer. I often ask people, "Do you go to church?" If they reply, "No," I like to ask them why. I try to gain some insight into what prevents people from participating in communal prayer. The most common answer I receive is "Church is boring." Sometimes I probe a little deeper by asking, "Do you pray?" Very often the same people reply, "No." When I ask them why they do not pray, they often reply, "Prayer is boring too."

I am not exaggerating in the slightest when I say that to pray each day is as important to me as it is to breathe. On days when I have neglected my prayer, I have felt peace and serenity evaporate and anxiety and worry increase, on both a physical and a spiritual level; my joy fades, and my ability to love with patience decreases. At first it astounded me to hear so many "intelligent people" proclaiming what used to belong only to young children and rebellious adolescents. How is it that so many people now firmly believe that prayer, whether conducted in private or in communion at church, is boring?

Can all of these people be wrong? Have they all been misled? Are they all liars? Or do they have a valid point? I have no doubt that they are indeed bored. But the question remains: *why* are they bored?

Their attitude will perhaps give us some insight into why we too do not pray or why we do not pray consistently. Let us look at this example.

Say, for instance, Fred went to church on a given Sunday some time ago. He actively participated in the Mass, and while he was in church that day the Lord spoke to him, not in an audible voice but in the very depths of Fred's heart.

By whatever means he chose, the Lord showed Fred that if he really wanted to be happy he was going to have to work on a certain area of his life, fix some relationship problems he was having, and stop doing certain other things.

Fred went away from church that week and ignored what God had told him.

The next week when Fred came back to church God said to him, "Are you any happier this week?"

"Not really," Fred replied.

Then God asked, "Fred, are you happy at all?"

Fred replied, "Well, I'm relatively happy, God."

"Relative to what?" God asked. "You have never known any greater happiness, so how do you know that you are happy at all?"

Then God went on to say, "Fred, do you remember last week I gave you lesson one and told you if you really want to be happy you are going to have to fix this, work on this, and stop doing this?" Fred heard what God said, but again he went away and throughout the week ignored the message.

He went back to church the next week, and what did God tell Fred? The same thing He told him the week before and the week before that: lesson one. Again Fred went away and during the week his words and actions ignored what God had said. But he continued to go to church, and what did God tell him? Lesson one, over and over.

My point is this: is it any wonder some people are bored? After all, they have been having lesson one every Sunday morning at ten o'clock for their whole lives.

The first reason why we don't pray—and why we often get bored if we do—is that we don't want to hear what God has to say. The problem is not that God is not speaking. It is that we are not listening.

The benefits of prayer come not from praying but from living what we discover in prayer. So many people at one time or another begin to pray. Each day they say their prayers, and this makes them feel good about themselves. But after a while saying their prayers becomes just another habit, and they do not get the same positive and affirming feelings from doing it; often they stop praying at that point. Many people falsely believe that if you pray, God will bless you.

God will bless you if you live what you discover in prayer, because when we live what we discover in prayer we become one with God. And when we are one with God, all that is His becomes ours.

STARTING OUT

The best forms of prayer are simple. Once upon a time there was a milkman in a small town in France. Each day he would spend considerable time sitting in the same pew near the back of a small church. One day out of curiosity the priest asked him what he did there each day. The man replied, "I look at the good God and the good God looks at me."

Simplicity is the key to perfection.

In the last four years, my life and attitudes have changed considerably. My focus has changed from an emphasis on "getting ahead" to one on growing and becoming. The experience of hearing God speak to me has been a great joy in my life, but this experience did not change my life. Prayer changed my life.

Consistent prayer transforms our lives.

When the Father began to call me to prayer, I wondered how to pray. He encouraged me to see Jesus as a friend. Each day I would go to my local church and spend some time in the presence of Jesus. At first it was for ten minutes a day. As time went by I increased the time I spent in prayer.

At first I would just sit there in the church and think about all the things that were going to happen that day; I would plan my future or daydream. I had made a commitment to myself to go for ten minutes every day to pray, but I soon came to see that I was not praying at all. This time in the quiet of the church cleared my mind and gave me time to plan my day, but it wasn't really prayer. Prayer is a dialogue. It requires an effort and a desire to grow.

On many occasions the Father spoke to me, encouraging me to engage in a gentle mental conversation with Christ.

*"Go today and sit in front of the tabernacle
and speak to My Son Jesus. Tell Him about all
your worries and fears, and He will remove
all your anxieties. Tell Him about your plans for
the day and the joys and the problems you
expect to encounter. Too many of you only tell
Him of problems. Many beautiful things are happening; share them with Him in prayer. Speak to
Him about everything that is happening in your
life. As your friend, He wants to know."*

Too often we see Jesus as just the candy man. We rush
into church, we kneel in the very last pew, and we say,
"Listen up, God, your servant is speaking. I want this
. . . , and I want this . . . , and I want this . . . , and I asked
for this . . . last week and you haven't given it to me yet.
And by the way, could you help Aunt Susan find her
cat?" Then we rush straight back out of the church. This
is not prayer. If you had a friend and you only saw that
friend when he came to ask you for money, would you
consider that person much of a friend?

The Father is calling us to a relationship with Jesus—
Jesus, who is the Way, the Truth, and the Life; Jesus who
is true God, true man, and true friend.

In one of the messages God the Father said, "All the
answers are in the tabernacle." Jesus has all the answers. How often we come to one of our friends and
say, "I've got this problem. . . . This is the situation. . . .
These are the circumstances. . . . What do you think I
should do?"

When was the last time you were faced with a problem and you decided to ask Jesus for His advice? You

do this in the same way you would ask any friend. Sit with the Lord and say, "Lord, I have this problem. This is the situation.... These are the circumstances.... What do you think I should do, Lord?" Explain the problem to Jesus as clearly and completely as you can, and then listen. Yes, listen. I am not saying that you will hear an audible voice, but I am sure that in some way God will lead you, direct you, and answer you. He may just tell you to be patient or to wait. He may inspire you to take some action. However He chooses to communicate with you, you will find peace if you listen carefully and follow the inspirations of your prayer.

Peace is the proof that God is present in your plans.

Slowly but surely I began to develop this relationship with Jesus. Each day, then as now, I stop at a church wherever I am and spend some time with Jesus. Most days this is not too difficult, but on some occasions it is not possible for me to visit a church, so I simply find a quiet place wherever I am and pray. For some people it is almost impossible to visit a church every day for this quiet time of prayer. We must adopt a pattern of prayer that matches our situation in life. Mothers of young children, for example, may find it difficult to get ten minutes of quiet *anywhere*. But somewhere, somehow we must pray each day. God understands our circumstances and always rewards our sincere efforts to know Him.

I begin my prayer by affirming my belief that Jesus is present and that He sees and hears me. Then I continue to speak to Him in a mental conversation just as I would speak to a good friend. I tell Him about my worries, and

He seems to lift the weight from my heart. I tell Him about my plans, my dreams, my friends, my family, my travels, and anything that is weighing on my heart or mind. I ask Him to point out to me my mistakes and faults. Most important, I speak to Him about decisions I need to make.

Toward the end of my prayer time I try to make one resolution for that day. Sometimes I make the same resolution for days and even weeks. Once I have finished my time of prayer, I ask Jesus for the strength and grace to live that resolution. Then at night before I go to bed I examine myself in the area of the resolution I made.

I try to continue this conversation with Jesus throughout the day. I invite Him to join me in my various activities. When I am traveling and speaking, I particularly like to take a walk each day. I find this to be a wonderful opportunity for conversation with Jesus. Prayer is about living in the presence of God. It doesn't have to be something that is confined to a few moments each day. By recognizing that "God is with us" before we begin each task, our lives become one continuous road to Emmaus.

I challenge you to ask yourself this question today and every day. What is my relationship with Jesus like today? Is it a friendship? Does it need work? Do you need to make amends? Is it consistent? Do you only come to Jesus when you want something?

Jesus is your friend; He has all the answers and desires a personal relationship with you. Sometimes friendship means talking, and sometimes it means listening. It is wisdom to know the difference. Prayer is not about all sorts of fancy petitions and sayings. Prayer is not a psychological mind game. It is an action of love that takes place between the spirit within you and the Spirit of God.

Sometimes when we are with a friend, it is not necessary for either person to speak. It is comforting, refreshing, and renewing just to be with that person. And so it is in our relationship with God.

—⁓—

Once there was a boy named Timmy. Christmas was coming around, and Timmy had decided that he wanted a bicycle more than anything else in the world. So he decided that he would write God a letter.

"Dear God," he wrote. "If you bring me a bicycle for Christmas, I promise I will be a good boy for one whole year. Love, Timmy." But Timmy looked at the letter and thought that it would be too hard to fulfill his side of the deal, so he ripped the letter into pieces and wrote God another letter, saying, "Dear God, if you bring me a bicycle for Christmas, I promise I will be a good boy for six months." But he didn't like this letter either. So he began again, writing, "Dear God, if you bring me a bicycle for Christmas, I promise I will wash the dishes every day for three months. Love, Timmy." But he looked at this letter and still thought this was too much. So Timmy decided to stop writing letters and look for other ways to get his bicycle.

The following Sunday, as always, Timmy's parents took him to church. As Timmy walked into the church he saw a small beautiful statue of Mary the Mother of God up on the side altar. Now, Timmy had seen the statue many times before. But it was on this Sunday that the statue touched him in a special way.

When Mass was finished Timmy asked his parents if he could stay behind and walk home alone. They only lived down the block, so his parents agreed. When everyone else had left the church, Timmy got up and walked to the front where the statue was. Standing before Mary he smiled and then, turning around to make sure there was nobody else there, he reached up and took the statue down. He carried the statue home and put it in his bedroom under his bed.

Then Timmy wrote God another letter, "Dear God, I've got your mother. Bring me my bicycle. It wouldn't be much of a Christmas without your mother. Love, Timmy."

Is your relationship with God like this? Are you always trying to strike a deal with God, trying to bribe Him? But God is calling you to a friendship.

MAKING TIME

We live in a busy world, a world full of entertainment and distractions. It is so easy for us to lose our focus unless we make a consistent effort, through prayer, to remain in touch with what is really important.

For a soul concerned with growing and experiencing the adventure of the inner journey, prayer must be an important priority.

It is so easy to wake up in the morning, rush into the day, and be swallowed up by the world. When we finally come home late at night, we remember, "Oh, I didn't pray today." So we climb into bed and perhaps rattle off a few prayers to relieve our conscience, or we simply say, "Sorry, God, I didn't pray today," and go to sleep.

But if we would stay awake for a few moments longer, we would hear God speak to us in the depths of our hearts. And He would ask, "Why didn't you pray today?" Then we would have to reply, "Well, God, you know how it is, I didn't pray today because I spent the whole day, the twenty-four hours for which you sustained my existence and which you filled with plentiful gifts, doing *everything that means nothing unless I've prayed.*"

We so often consider ourselves to be wise—yet we act like fools. The journey of the soul is about setting priorities. In His preaching Jesus set these priorities before us: God, family, friends, work. Unfortunately the corporation and the dollar have risen to top priority for so many of us. We are more concerned with our careers or with our financial security than we are with the God who created us, who sustains us, and who fills our lives with abundant gifts. And not only does He do all of this but He promises more through prayer.

> **Without God in your life, your long-term career prospects are not looking good at all, and you have no security, financial or otherwise. We often neglect prayer because we are too caught up with other aspects of our lives. It is not that we don't have time. The problem is that we don't give prayer a high enough priority.**

Once when I was speaking in Canada, I asked my audience this question, "If I put a hundred million dollars on the ground in front of you and told you if you come back tomorrow you can each take a thousand dollars, who wouldn't come back?"

One humorous man in the audience spoke up, saying that he wouldn't come back because a thousand dollars wasn't enough. The audience laughed and I continued, "Very well, then, if I put the same hundred million dollars here on the floor and told you that if you come here sometime tomorrow, you could have ten thousand dollars each, who wouldn't come back?" The same man exclaimed, "I wouldn't go home." Again we all laughed.

Supposing I put that money in your church and told you that if you went to visit your local church tomorrow and spent ten minutes in prayer you could take ten thousand dollars. Would you make it to your church tomorrow if you knew ten thousand dollars were waiting for you?

Most of us are busy people with a lot of things to do. But for ten thousand dollars we'd find time. For ten thousand dollars we'd *make* time, we would give it top priority—but visiting Jesus, who is our greatest friend, who has all the answers, and who will set our minds at ease, is not important enough to go out of our way. Has money become our God? For how long will we continue to neglect prayer?

To most people in the world today, time is an extremely important and valuable commodity. People value their time above all other things and regard it as something not to be wasted. Yet even with this incredible emphasis on getting things done quickly and on not wasting any time, we tend to waste a huge amount each day. Procrastination is a disease that is still rampant in the workplace, in the university, and just about any-place where people need to get something done. We waste time by shuffling papers instead of writing them, by daydreaming instead of making dreams come true—there are countless examples of ways we waste time each day.

If we find each day coming to a close and we have not found time for prayer, perhaps we need to partake in a simple time-management study. The first question we need to ask ourselves is, how have I spent my time today? What have I done? What is it that I have done in this twenty-four-hour period that was so much more important than spending time with God?

In examining how we use our time, perhaps we should begin with the one-eyed monster. Yes, television. If you sit before a TV on any day before you have spent time in prayer, you commit a grave injustice against yourself. Television is the thief of love. I have seen the diabolical fruits of television all over the world. I have seen its effects on all levels of society, in rich people's homes and in poor people's homes. I have seen children, young children and not-so-young children, come rushing into the house full of happiness and excitement because something wonderful has happened to them during the day, and I've seen them be brushed aside because a parent was in the middle of a television program. "Not now," the parents say, and the child is crushed like a melon under the wheel of a truck. Love is now.

Television is the thief of love because television kills communication; communication leads to understanding; and understanding breeds love.

Be very careful about the role you allow television to play in your life and in the lives of those you love. Being concerned with the life of the soul is about being countercultural. It is about expanding the mind beyond the things of the material realm. The television and the world are concerned with the body and the temporal. The television and the media create and sustain culture. They don't publish what is countercultural because they believe that too few are interested.

———

Prayer is the key to all the deepest desires of our hearts. In prayer God reveals the secrets that humanity longs to know. In prayer God reveals to us the plan for happiness that He holds for us. In prayer He nourishes us and fills us with hope, giving us strength to continue along the journey.

If there were a little more peace, joy, love, and happiness in your heart tomorrow, would you have a better day? And if there were a little more peace, joy, love, and happiness in your family tomorrow, would it be a better family? And if there were a little more peace, joy, love, and happiness in your friendships tomorrow, would they be better friendships? And if there were a little more peace, joy, love, and happiness in your workplace tomorrow, would it be a better workplace? And is not the world made up of people who are not only individuals but also members of families, people who have friendships and who go to work? So imagine the peace, joy, love, and happiness that you would be a part of and surrounded by.

Pray. Pray. Peace, joy, love, and happiness are the fruits of prayer. Prayer is important. The world needs men and women who are able to resist the ever-present pressures to dilute the ideal that surround us at every level of society. Such men and women will place prayer at the absolute center of their lives.

Make a resolution today to pray each day. There are hundreds of ways to pray. Decide on one now and apply it to your life. Give it top priority.

Ten minutes a day in prayer can change your life more radically than you could ever imagine.

If for the next ten days you will wake up, shower, have breakfast, and then before you do anything else, spend ten minutes in prayer, your life will begin to take on a unity that will bring serenity and peace. And this serenity and peace will have practical results, giving you a calm levelheadedness that will in turn make you much more effective.

God is happy. In fact, God is happiness. Our happiness is dependent on whether or not we actively move to unite ourselves with God. The task of humanity is to become one with God. The attainment of everything good that we desire for ourselves, our neighbor, and our world is dependent on our becoming one with God. We become one with God by raising our hearts and minds to truth, goodness, and the things of the spiritual realm. We become one with God in prayer—and so our life itself should be a prayer.

God calls us to prayer to participate in and stimulate the inner life. He calls us in order to turn on the tap of our spiritual lives. He doesn't want us to turn the tap on so hard that the water comes gushing out. No, He just wants us to turn the tap on to a steady drip. Visualize this dripping tap.

If you place a bucket under a dripping tap, eventually the bucket will fill. And once the bucket is full, the water will overflow. It has to overflow.

The tap is the spiritual life. The mind, the will, and the intellect turn the tap on. The drops of water clean and refresh. The drops of water are peace, joy, love, and happiness. The bucket is our heart, our soul. Drop by drop we are filled with these fruits of prayer. Once we are full, they have to overflow.

The secret is to pray consistently and perseveringly, like the dripping tap. Remember:

No vase can overflow if you never fill it up.

CHAPTER 5

NOW

The present moment feeds, nourishes, educates, instructs, guides, counsels, loves, and sanctifies.

A YOUNG man on a long car trip with his father broke the silence to say, "Dad, I'll be happy when I have security for my wife and children." The father sighed and said, "My boy, we only ever have one moment of happiness and that is the present moment, yet we are constantly surrendering it for some greater happiness that is always just out of our reach and eventually is stolen from us by death." The young man marveled at his father's wisdom while his father appreciated the landscape; then the older man continued, "Son, recognize that *you* are happiness. Then begin to share it with your wife, and children, and everyone you meet. The more you bring happiness to others, the more you will recognize the infinite treasure of happiness within you."

The father was a very wealthy man and had owned and managed over forty large companies at one time. A few minutes of silence passed before the son said to his father, "When I was young, Dad, and you were right at the core of the business world, you were happy. Now you've retired and generally the pace is much slower, and you still seem happy. From the fast pace of the business world to the slower pace of the social world and from your dealings with the media to dealing with family life and retired life, what is your secret for being happy in the moment?"

Smiling, the father said, "Do you remember when you were eleven and you made the grand final of the soccer competition?" The son nodded, and the older man continued, "In the middle of that game a report was going to be released that would either make me a considerably wealthier man or throw me into debt. But it didn't matter where I was at the time of the announcement; there was absolutely nothing I could do before or after it was made that I hadn't taken care of that morning in the office. And so I stood on the sidelines with my eyes glued to you, watching every kick, run, tackle, and move you made. My thoughts departed only occasionally to think of your mother and the wonderful times we had together while she was carrying you in her womb. I thought of the first time I held you in my arms and the first time you walked. From the sidelines my whole attention and every thought were focused on you. From the sidelines I spent my time and my energies for sixty minutes loving you. It is this concentration that has been my greatest tool in becoming a rich man both in material things and in love."

The young man, a little impatient and slow to understand, persisted, "Yes, Dad, but what's your secret?"

Slowly, with a calm, steady, loving look, the father then replied, "I am where I am."

———

Somewhere in this story is hidden a divine call to love. A call from God to love as He loves. A call to demonstrate a universal love. A call to recognize that the life force in all the other people and things around us is the same life force that is within us. A call to love all things as God loves them in the present moment. All you need do is recognize that you have the ability to allow God to work through you and bring happiness to others. And the more you give happiness to others, the more you will have for yourself.

Practically, this means giving your attention to the person, or people, you are with and the environment you are in at the present moment.

So often we spend our days living in the past or the future—worrying, regretting, dreaming, predicting. At the same time life is passing us by. But life, every moment of it, is precious.

If we could only be where we are and allow ourselves to become intoxicated by the love of God in that moment, how much more of life we would take in and how much happier we would be.

How long has it been since you took a really close look at a flower and appreciated its amazing complexity and beauty?

Next time you see a flower, look at it and appreciate it. Focus on the colors, shapes, and aroma of the flower. Then look at it with the love God has for it as He sustains its life. This simple exercise will help you to notice the richness and beauty of life in all its many forms. When you have learned to stop and notice, appreciate and love the flower as a rich, complex, and beautiful part of creation, your ability to love and appreciate the next person you meet will be radically increased. For what is a flower compared to a person?

The secret lies in this thought: "I am where I am and I love where I am." It is not that we have to like every place we go, but wherever we go, whatever we do, we should spend our energies loving. Our happiness lies in expending our energies in loving the people, places, and all forms of life that present themselves to us in any given moment; we do this by recognizing that their life and beauty have been given and are sustained by God.

There are many states of mind that prevent us from living in the present moment, but the one that dominates almost every human heart is lack of trust.

Trust and an understanding of self-worth are the two things that lead to happiness, and they are the most basic principles of Christianity. Yet they are the very things we kill.

When someone cannot trust, when someone feels worthless, how can that person be happy?

Our lack of trust extends not only to other people and to material circumstances but ultimately to God. We do not trust God. And because we do not trust God, we are unable to live in the present moment. Fears and worries fester in our minds and weigh heavily on our hearts, preventing us from experiencing and enjoying the wonder of now.

We are living in a sad period of history when it is common to hear someone say to a child, "Don't trust anybody." Today even many of the people of God don't seem to trust God. Perhaps we should examine the way previous generations with these attitudes have ended up. There seems to be a contraceptive mentality that is spreading throughout the world. I am referring to something greater than the fact that more and more people are using contraceptives to prevent pregnancy. Still, if we look at this one example of the contraceptive mentality, perhaps it will illustrate what I mean.

Our ability to take part in the reproduction of human life is a special gift from God. Such an act is meant to be a cooperation with God. The use of contraception cuts God out of the act, tries to prevent God from working through this natural and beautiful process, and thus reduces sexual intercourse to nothing but the satisfaction of desires. The idea of cutting God out of certain situations occurs in many other aspects of contemporary life. Always, this runs against nature and can hardly be beneficial for the persons involved or for humanity as a whole.

This whole contraceptive mentality denies divine providence and leads people to trust God less and less. They no longer feel the need to pray and discover God's plan. Thus they become more and more unhappy as their attachments to the material world increase and their soul's ability to soar to great heights is greatly reduced.

Our happiness and our surrender to God in all things are linked, but surrender is slow, painful, and often a struggle. It is most beneficial and necessary for us to surrender our plans and ambitions to God. This surrender frees us of our worries and anxieties, which are the result of attachment to our ambitions and their material consequences. When we trust in God, we become less attached to the material world, the spirit begins to soar, and we grow in happiness—true happiness.

Jesus as the fullness of revelation came to show us all things so that we could imitate Him in our own lives. Through His incarnation He descended on the earth, and while remaining God, He took on all the conditions of our human state. He was thus a unique composition of divinity and humanity. Jesus walked the path of this life growing and learning in all human ways just as you and I do. His journey climaxed in His ascension into Heaven, and it was this that He ultimately came to show us: the way to the Father. His Crucifixion and death were necessary for our redemption but were not the only reason for His coming among us. Jesus came to show us the way to ascend to God the Father. After His ascension He then sent His Spirit into the world to lead us along the path toward God.

His death and resurrection brought us to life, life in the Spirit. When we sin, we reject this life in the Spirit. Life in the Spirit is living the now.

The Spirit is joy. When we sin, we choose misery and reject joy.

When we become excessively attached to the things of this world, we abandon the peace that comes from life in the Spirit and fall into the animal-like slavery from which Christ came to set us free.

It is by increasing our efforts to walk this path with Christ that we grow in happiness. This path is the path of salvation and is dependent on our surrender to God. God wants everything from each of us, but you do not surrender everything to someone you do not know. So He is calling us to pray, to get to know Him a little more. The more we get to know Him, the more we will be able to trust Him and the more we will be prepared to surrender ourselves to Him.

Communication begets knowledge. Knowledge begets trust. Trust begets surrender. Surrender begets happiness.

When we surrender the future to God and trust in His providence in every sense, we are able to enjoy and benefit completely from the now. But this surrender involves not only detaching ourselves from material things but also detaching from the standards and ideals of the world. The latter detachment often leads us to experience the same hostility from the people around us that Christ experienced when He wouldn't conform to the standards of the world. Surrender, which in itself is a wonderful thing and is beneficial for our personal growth and ascent toward God, often leads to a kind of rejection, allowing us to share in Christ's experience on the cross. Pain is powerful, and experience is an effective teacher.

Thus we walk the path of salvation, and while the world stands bewildered at the will of God, those who dare to take the step revealed to them will find the next just as clear as soon as they take the first. Step by step we are led to our fulfillment, perfection, and completion along the path by which a human being ascends toward God the Father. It is this fulfillment and the struggle to perfect our soul that bring happiness to our lives and give glory to God.

In Jesus Christ, God became man, and thus the fullness of truth was revealed to humanity. All previous philosophies were confirmed or disproved by Christ's life and teaching, so philosophy was elevated to its completion, and all limitations that previously inhibited humanity were lifted. As well as bringing changes to our understanding, the coming of Christ also brought changes to our existence as human beings, for the weight of our sins was removed from our shoulders and we were taught to hope in the joy of eternal life. This joy begins partially in this life and is brought to its fulfillment in the next. It is this joy of redemption and this hope of eternal life that have elevated and completed our happiness as human beings.

The amount of happiness that we experience in this life depends on what we focus on and how we spend our energies. For example, if we are forever focusing on material possessions or the lack of them and committing all types of injustices against our neighbor, however small they may be, then we can hardly expect to be happy. Why? Because these actions directly oppose truth. These actions oppose the gospel, and true happiness will never be found in sin or falsehood.

However, if we learn to appreciate all the many gifts we have and to love our neighbor in word and action, then we will live in the now and be happy. To learn to appreciate our gifts, we simply have to acknowledge how much we have all been given in the material realm as well as the infinite opportunity we are offered in the spiritual realm. Did not Christ say, "He who has much will be given even more and he who has little, even that will be taken from him"? When we don't appreciate what we have, we are robbed even of the joy of the little we have by the desire to have more and by all the associated anxieties this desire brings. The opposite is also true: when we take time to thank God for His gifts and appreciate them, our happiness expands. Appreciation is the multiplier of gifts. One of the greatest tools for living in and learning from the present moment is appreciation. To learn to love our neighbor, we need only remember that what we do to others we do to ourselves.

THE FRUIT OF APPRECIATION

I woke up this morning and got out of bed. Now, that might not strike you as being anything too extraordinary, because you probably do it every day, but there are thousands of people who did not get out of bed this morning. Many because they didn't have a bed to get out of, others because of sickness or disability, and still others because they died during the night. But I got up out of bed this morning, and then I had a nice shower with hot clean water. There are millions of people in the world today who don't have clean water to drink, never mind clean hot water to wash with. Then I got dressed and I put clean clothes on. My wardrobe includes many clothes, yet I wonder how many people in the world are wearing the same clothes today that they wore yesterday, and the day before, and for weeks and months, because these are the only clothes they have. Then I went downstairs and ate breakfast. I wonder how many millions of people have nothing to eat today, how many of them are starving to death. I can read and write. I have friends and family who love and care for me. I have things to dream about and things to look forward to. . . .

Sometimes we feel that there is a void in our lives. We associate this void with a lack of happiness. We tell ourselves, "If only I could do this, or have that, or if only I could be that, then I would be happy and this void would disappear." We are wrong. The problem is we are forever focusing on all the things we cannot do, all the things we do not have, and all the people that we are not.

Joy is the fruit of appreciation.

When we take a few moments each day to reflect in silence on who we are, on the talents we have, and on the many wonderful gifts and people that fill our lives, we begin to dance for joy.

If you want to know what to pray about or what to meditate on, this is it: the gifts in your life. Most of them are simple things that we take for granted every day.

For ten minutes close your eyes and imagine that you have no legs. How would this affect the way you live your life? What would be the inconveniences? At the end of your meditation, you will have renewed respect and appreciation for your legs.

The saddest thing in the world is wasted talent. Recognize your gifts. Appreciate them. Then you will use them wisely.

We tend to live in the poets' realm: we only learn to appreciate people and things when they are lost or gone. When we get sick, we appreciate the good health we once had. How many people only learn of their over-whelming love for their parents after their parents have died? Why? Because so many of us do not stop to appreciate the many wonderful things our parents and others do for us in our lives. When our loved ones die, their absence forces us to recognize all that they have done and been.

Reflect appreciatively on the gifts and people in your life.

I can see now that when I have experienced unhappiness in my life, it was most often caused not by a lack of something but because I did not enjoy what I had at that moment.

I can see now that when I have felt lonely and not loved, it was not because I was all alone and that no one loved me but because I was rejecting the people God was sending into my life as companions and instead I was desiring to be with others.

The present moment feeds, nourishes, educates, instructs, guides, counsels, loves, and sanctifies.

No other prayer will fill you with greater joy than a prayer of gratitude. Recognize what you have.

When you pray today, put the prayers you say each day aside and just thank God—for life, for the people in your life, for the talents you have, for roses and daisies, for birds and koala bears, for the sun and the sea, the stars and the moon, for water and wind, for fire and rain, for the special moments you have had, the lessons you have learned, the heartaches you have come through, for music and for books, for freedom, for your country, for your mother and father, brothers and sisters, friends, your job, your children, the money you have, the place where you live, the car that you drive, the air that you breathe. . . .

We only have little when we are unappreciative. If you don't appreciate something, you do not really have it because you do not have the joy it offers.

Any relationship depends vitally on appreciation. You cannot love someone you do not appreciate. Love is our response to a truth realized. We realize something is beautiful; in other words, we recognize the truth that something is beautiful. Our response to this truth is our love for that something. You come to know that a person is sincere. You recognize this sincerity as a manifestation of truth and goodness. You appreciate that sincerity. Your response to this truth in that person is love.

However, appreciation is an acquired art and virtue. Like anything good, it must be sought. To discover truth is not enough. Many discover it but then despise it. Others, the wiser, discover it and then appreciate it, love it, and try to fill their lives with it.

Appreciation, love, and reverence are all linked. We love those things we appreciate, and we revere those things we love. But in our lives there is not enough appreciation, there is not enough love, and therefore there is not enough reverence. We must change this, and to do so requires an active response and an effort.

Look around you now, wherever you are. Do you see a plant, an animal, or a person? Focus your attention on one of these for a moment. In these things there is life—

the inexplicable mystery of life. I cannot see the plant on my desk move, but I know that it is alive and it grows. I do not know the details of how or why, but I know of an infinite Creator who sustains the life of that plant. The same Creator who sustains the life of the plant sustains my life and yours. We pass by these almost unfathomable mysteries without even noticing them hundreds of times a day. So today when you look at people, really look at them; go beyond their imperfections and failings, for when you recognize the mystery of life within them, you will see beauty, you will see truth, you will appreciate them, you will love them, you will revere them.

The secret to lasting happiness and success in anything is recognizing and remembering where the gifts come from.

It is this appreciation that is lacking in our relationship with God. We need to take a closer look at God. He illustrates His magnificence in His creation, yet creation is only a dim reflection of the God who created it. When we appreciate God and all He has freely given us, we will love Him, and our love for Him will express itself in reverence.

It is this appreciation that our human relationships need. Watch your spouse cook a meal or hang out the wash or go to work or wash the car, watch your children as they do their chores or their homework, watch your parents as they walk together. . . . These people are a part of your life. They are wonderful, they are beautiful. Learn to appreciate them a little more, and you will be able to love them more. And your love for them will express itself in a renewed reverence and respect for them. Life is to be appreciated. Life is lovable and life should be reverenced.

Not only is joy the fruit of appreciation but when we appreciate the gifts God has given us He multiplies them.

The dance continues and becomes even more intense as we develop this sense of appreciation. Joy is the fruit of appreciation.

Joy is not about having something but about appreciating what you have. You could have the whole world and every good thing, but if you do not appreciate them, you will not experience joy.

THE DANCE

We all have the ability to dance for joy. Perhaps it feels easy to dance in the midst of abundance and to dance when everything seems to be going all right; perhaps we can even learn to dance in the midst of turmoil and pressure—but what about illness?

Dancing for joy is a response to the inner freedom that comes from struggling to discover and live the truth. When I am sincere about this struggle, I feel this inner freedom—this is my joy. Thus, when I speak of dancing for joy, I do not mean that joy is the absence of pain and suffering.

In fact, this joy I speak of is not the happiness of a healthy or happy person but is rather a much greater supernatural reality. When I speak of joy, I am speaking of a state of mind and a condition of the heart that allow us to focus on a higher reality. The higher reality is the eternity of the soul and the soul's supreme reign over the body. And we can focus on this higher reality even when—perhaps especially when—we are sick.

Yet very often we let our busy lives and our bodies prevent us from growing spiritually.

When we are involuntarily slowed down by illness, we are provided with plenty of time to pray, reflect, contemplate, make resolutions, and seek new direction in our lives.

Some people do not deal well with sickness. They are impatient. They seem constantly agitated, and this agitation is put down to the sickness, but it is really a reflection of a deeper problem. In sickness we face ourselves in much the same way that we face ourselves when we pray. Sickness provides a certain detachment from our bodies; it offers the stillness that we try to achieve in prayer. Sickness also reminds us of our nothingness and dependence on God.

When we refuse to slow down and we let our fast-paced lives drive us to illness, our impatience reflects our unwillingness to face the truth about ourselves. Then we are not seeking holiness with our lives. We are not trying to find the truth, we are trying to avoid it. We avoid the truth about ourselves, our lives, and our God by the use of all sorts of distractions, entertainment, pleasure, and possessions. So we cage ourselves in, chain ourselves up, and call it freedom—freedom to ignore and avoid the truth. It is an exercise of freedom, but it does not free us.

When we begin to search for truth and live truth, then slowly we develop the awareness that every circumstance in our lives has been designed to teach us a certain truth. We learn to seek the truth that the moment wishes to bestow. In this frame of mind, we are able to recognize illness as an opportunity. This attitude doesn't take away the pain—sometimes nothing can—but it does bring meaning to the pain.

Often an illness can be our passport to a higher state.

Little by little we discover truth and allow it to emerge in our lives. Gradually we become aware of God's presence within us, and we begin to dance for joy. This joy begins to permeate all the activities of our days.

FALSE IMAGES OF GOD

Once I had discovered all of this, there came a point when I experienced a strange confusion. I recognized this joy as the presence of God in my life, but this conflicted with my previous understanding of God. Many people had told me that God was a God of punishment, the inflicter of suffering, a harsh God ruling with an iron rod, the God of rules and regulations. Now I was learning that the God they had proclaimed was no God at all.

Our God is the God of infinite mystery and wonder. His gift is joy. His favorite pastime is dancing for joy with His sons and daughters. And God—above all else, before all else, and in the midst of all else—is love.

FRIENDSHIP

Friends are important in the journey of the soul and particularly when it comes to grasping the now. Good friends lead us to use the present moment wisely. True friends have our best interests at heart, and our best interests are those of the soul.

Friendship is a miracle.

How would we define friends? Two people who share something in common—something great or small, a joy or a sadness, a dream or an affection, or perhaps some knowledge.

We bond with others in friendship despite our complexes and biases that have been formed by past experiences. This is indeed a miracle. And through this miracle God caters to many of our natural and supernatural needs, such as our need to share, to speak, to listen, to laugh, to be listened to, to cry, to be held by another, to hold another, to be understood and to understand, to care for another and be cared for by another, to forgive and be forgiven, to love and be loved, to lead others to God and to be led to God by others.

Friendship is a treasure to be cherished.

Our friends, whether we are prepared to admit it or not, have a tremendous influence on us. If you surround yourself with great people, you will become a great person. If you surround yourself with people who are striving for academic excellence, you will develop the hunger for academic excellence. If you surround yourself with people who constantly see themselves as victims in the game of life, you will take on the mentality of a victim, and you will become a victim. If you surround yourself with people who are heroically struggling to better themselves and to grow in the image of God, you will develop the hunger to do the same, and you too will grow in the image of God.

You will learn more from your friends than you ever will from books. Choose your friends wisely and make Jesus the first.

God attends to so many of our needs through friendship, but it is also true that friendship can be abused. When a friendship is wholesome and its ultimate goal is to lead each other to the fulfillment and happiness that God desires for us, then it is a positive experience and a wonderful gift. Such friendships should be protected and cherished, for they are rare. When this is not the goal of a friendship, beware, for such a friendship promises something it can never give. Friendships of this nature are limited to the material and physical realm, and, far from elevating our consciousness to the spiritual realm, they limit our focus to the things of the world. And the things of this world promise a happiness they cannot deliver. Happiness is the explosion that takes place when we carefully mix the things of this world with our life in the Spirit.

Once we have accepted that our happiness is dependent on change and on the growth that comes from change, then we will see the need to surround ourselves with people who also understand the need for change in their lives. Unfortunately, as we begin to change, we may find ourselves in a lonely place. Often the friends we had prior to accepting the need and challenge to change no longer want to be around us, because our example challenges them to change or because we no longer want to be involved in the activities that take place when such friends get together.

Most of us surround ourselves with people who demand so little of us. We surround ourselves with people who won't challenge us to change and grow, because we desire comfort and social acceptance. We desire this type of comfort because we think it will make us happy. We are wrong. This type of comfort does not lead us to fulfillment and therefore does not make us happy. Such comfort is a pleasure, but it is completely limited to the time we spend with these friends; when we are alone, we experience an emptiness because we are not striving for or experiencing fulfillment.

Our friends have a tremendous influence on the people we become.

We become what we love.

If we love things that are good and noble, we become good and noble. If we love things that are evil and destructive, we become evil and destructive. If we love, admire, and spend time with people who are happy and striving for fulfillment, then we will become like them. Friendship is a wonderful gift designed, like family, to assist us and encourage us along the path of salvation, happiness, and fulfillment, toward union with God.

If you are my friend, do these three things for me: teach me to love; teach me to be loved; and lead me to God.

AN OVERFLOW OF JOY

As this dance for joy begins to develop within us, it isn't something that we can switch on and off; it becomes a part of us and is sustained by prayer, the sacraments, and reflection on the gifts with which God has filled our daily lives. Wherever we go, whomever we are with, whatever we do, this joy overflows, enriching other people's lives and influencing different environments and a variety of events. It is then that we are living the truth of Christian joy.

This joy is the by-product that fills our hearts, minds, and souls when the natural is carefully mixed with the supernatural. This joy is calm, serene, natural, and consistent because it is not linked to our emotions, feelings, possessions, nor to the changing events of our lives but rather it is the result of our union with God.

When we accept the present moment, we simultaneously reject worries and fears of the future, and we experience joy. Fears and worries rob us of the richness of the present moment. They steal the joy from our lives.

You come to me with that sad face, the worries of the world on your shoulders, and no trust in your Heavenly Father, and I cannot see Christ in you. Can you blame me?

One of the most easily identifiable characteristics of Christian happiness is its attractiveness. A selfish kind of happiness is not attractive; it is repulsive. Christian happiness, however, is tremendously attractive and very contagious.

If through our words and actions we intoxicate this world with happiness, then our homes, offices, churches, and social meeting places will begin to be transformed. We will begin to have more friends than ever before. Why? Because people like to be around people who are happy.

Others are attracted to the joy that comes from living in the now, and they want the same happiness for themselves. It is then that we are able to show them that Christ is the way; by leading them to Christ and this happiness, we are performing an apostolic task. We are spreading the faith. It is this personal apostolate of friend helping friend that Christianity so much needs; everyone has a need to be led closer to Christ, and everyone in the faith needs to share his or her faith with others. Nothing strengthens the faith of a soul like serving as an apostle.

Let the joy of knowing Christ, the joy of your soul, flow through you to someone else today. Extend the true hand of friendship and share your faith with another.

Too many people would have us believe that the perfume of God is pain and suffering. It is not. The perfume of God is happiness, and it is exactly this happiness that He wants for each of His children. This is the reason that we are called to pray and participate in the sacraments: so that we can discover the happiness of the Christian life, which is founded in our freedom and gained by our redemption.

Saint James tells us simply, "If you want to be happy, pray."

For those who love God, there is a question that always arises: what is the will of God? The will of God is that you be happy. Prayer increases our ability to accept the present moment. You cannot live in the future, you cannot live in the past, you can only live in the now.

The present moment is already exactly as it ought to be, even if we do not understand why it is as it is.

CHAPTER 6

SILENCE AND THE PRESENCE OF GOD

Silence is sacred.

OURS is a noisy world, full of symbols, words, messages, and communication. It is a loud and confusing place, and we have made it so.

People wake up in the morning to clock radios, listen to the news while they shower, watch television while they eat breakfast, get into the car and listen to the radio on the way to work, then listen to music all day over the intercom, and talk to people on the phone. . . . We need to STOP THE NOISE.

Noise is the mouthpiece of the material world. Silence is the mouthpiece of the supernatural realm. There is an evil in this world that we have created. It is evil because it separates us from God and therefore from everything good and because it leads to the destruction of our spirits. This evil is the continuous noise that we create for ourselves and for others. If we cannot hear the voice of God in our lives, it is not because He is not speaking; it is because we are drowning His voice out with so much other useless noise.

Silence is sacred and belongs not to this world but to the supernatural life. It is for this reason that people who spend time in silence are able to recognize supernatural realities while the eyes and ears of others remain closed.

The Scriptures say, "Be still and know I am God." If we will sit ourselves down quietly in one place for long enough, we will slowly come to see the wonders of the sacred. Silence is the language of the eternal.

We talk so much of love. We want to love and to be loved. The language of love is silence.

We also want wisdom. In our foolishness we think that wisdom will come from knowing practices or theories, so we read dozens of books. But God bestows His wisdom on men and women in the classroom of silence. May silence become a great friend of ours.

If you want to be wise, get to know yourself. After a knowledge of God, there is no greater practical wisdom than knowledge of self. And from this knowledge of self will flow the children of wisdom: humility, prudence, charity, and discretion.

It is true that there is much to be learned from other people's experiences, whether these have been victories or defeats, failures, mistakes, or successes, but experience is not the only teacher.

You can learn more in an hour of silence than you can in a year from books.

For the soul to be nourished adequately, we must spend time each day in silence. In this silence God leads, heals, renews, refreshes, directs, discloses, enlightens, and teaches us.

It is important for the journeying soul to create a place within. It must be a place of stillness where there is no noise. By spending time in silence, we encourage this place to grow. During this time, we must slow down our minds, dismiss all thoughts of the things of this world, and place our whole focus on God.

I like to sit still, close my eyes, and imagine a single red rose before me. The rose has long been a symbol for Christ. Fixing my attention on the beauty and splendor of the rose helps me to dismiss other mundane thoughts and allows my consciousness to be raised to the spiritual realm. On different days I experience varying degrees of success and varying types of distractions. What is important is that I make an effort to dismiss any distractions from my life and focus on the Divine.

It is this silence that brings me into the presence of God in a powerful way. Then throughout the rest of my day, I am still able to experience an interior silence and the presence of God, even though I am not experiencing exterior silence. God is always present; we simply do not recognize His presence because we are distracted by the noise of the world and the noise that we create within ourselves with useless thoughts and worrying. Prayer creates a quiet place within us where we can go at any time regardless of what is taking place around us. In this quiet place, we are constantly aware of God's presence, and His presence, inspiring us, flows through our words and action.

> **Silence is the best way to remember the presence of God. When we live in the presence of God, we dance for joy.**

In order to maintain this quiet place within us, we must protect it by practicing the virtue of silence. There is a time to speak and a time to remain silent. The virtue of silence lies in knowing the difference. Most of us talk too much. Often people in a group will never stop talking, not because anyone necessarily has anything important to say but because people feel that someone should be speaking. Most people are uncomfortable with silence.

And almost inevitably when there is a lull in the conversation, someone will begin to complain about something or slander someone.

> **Why do you complain so much? You complain about your husband, your wife, your mother, your father, your children, your friends, your work, the weather in the summer because it is too hot, and the weather in the winter because it is too cold. Do you not see how ridiculous and self-centered your complaints are?**

One of the ways to protect our quiet place within is to refrain from all useless discussion.

By practicing this self-restraint in speech and maintaining this quiet place within, we will always be aware of the presence of God. Then when we do speak, our words will break down the barriers between this world and the next. Words are the tools of the material world, while silence is the mystery of the spiritual realm. The person who is able to exist both in the supernatural realm and in the material realm by maintaining this quiet place within will bring the gifts of the supernatural world to this life.

A love of silence reflects a love for those things that are eternal. Silence is the surest and safest way to find our true selves and the fulfillment and joy we desire. A life that honors silence makes a person wise and virtuous.

God is the Giver. God never takes—He only gives. His gifts are always flowing. His blessings never cease, and God has no favorites. The Scriptures tell us He lets the sun shine on the wicked just as He lets it shine on the righteous. The difference is receptivity. How receptive are we to God's gifts? Do we use our natural capacities of the will and intellect to open ourselves up to the divine life to which God calls us?

Receptivity—an interesting concept. How receptive are you to God's grace? God poured forth grace in the same way for Hitler as He did for Francis of Assisi. The difference lay in their receptivity.

Silence increases our receptivity.

THOUGHTS

The key to the good use of each moment of the day, particularly the silent moments, is to control what we allow to occupy our minds. Our thoughts mold our lives.

If you reflect enough on bitter things, you will become bitter. If you reflect enough on joyful things, you will become joyful.

There is a mysterious strength to the human mind that we perhaps will never fully understand, but there are some things that we know that allow us to use this strength to our advantage. Nothing influences our words and actions more than what we allow to occupy our minds.

Saint Paul's advice is simple, practical, and profound: "Whatever is true, whatever is honorable, whatever is just, whatever is pure, whatever is pleasing, whatever is commendable, if there is any excellence and if there is anything worthy of praise, think about these things" (Philippians 4:8).

Once we decide to accept the challenge to change and grow and make the journey of the soul, we must keep our minds focused on what we are setting out to achieve. Prayer is a powerful instrument that assists us in maintaining this focus. It is during prayer that we bring to mind the things that we desire—things that are true, honorable, just, pure, pleasing, excellent, and worthy of praise. By doing so we set the compass of our soul and focus on the things of eternity.

This is why the best and most effective time to pray is first thing in the morning. Then our minds are usually not yet clogged with distractions and concerns. As we go through the day we take on board everything that happens and everything that people say to us. If we have set our focus in the morning through prayer, then we look at the events of the day from the perspective of prayer. If we pray later in the day, we often pray from the perspective of the events that have influenced our day.

Prayer influences and gives focus to the thoughts that fill our minds.

I remember that when I was a young boy saying good night to my parents on a Friday, my father would tell me to lie in bed and imagine a big win in my soccer game the next day. He wanted me to fill my mind with the goal I wished to achieve. When I was sixteen I spent a lot of time playing golf. One day I met a young professional golfer who gave me a few tips. One thing he said remains with me even now every time I swing a golf club. He told me, "Stand behind the ball before you hit each shot. Look at where the ball is and then at where you want the ball to go. Then imagine the shot you want to hit. If you can't imagine the shot, you can't hit the shot."

Human thought is creative. What we think becomes.

Positive thinking is a Christian principle. It was certainly not invented, or even discovered, by the businesspeople of this century. Every Christian should apply the methods of goal setting and positive thinking to their lives. Our long-term goal is to be one with God.

Our short-term goals are to change, to grow, to allow the image of God to emerge within us. The means we employ for achieving these goals are prayer, the sacraments, and our daily works. We should approach these goals with a positive mind, knowing that without God we are nothing but that we are not without God. And so with Him all things are possible. When we align our own will with His will, His strength and wisdom become available to us. We should ask for the wisdom to pray and the strength to live what we discover in prayer, and we should believe that these will be given to us.

> **Doubts, worries, and thoughts of disbelief block God from working in our lives. Faith and a mind that is set on hope welcome all the wondrous gifts God is waiting to bestow on us.**

In my life I have often had unanswered questions. Over the past three years I have learned to turn to Him who has all the answers and to ask Him to enlighten my mind. I ask Him to show me at the most appropriate moment what the answer or solution to my question is, and I believe that He will. And He does—always. I ask for light and light is given.

One of the passages from Scripture that I often reflect on is the one in which a blind man at the side of the road cries out to Jesus, who is passing by, "Jesus, Son of David, have mercy on me." The man is ignored and rebuked by the crowd and the disciples, but he cries all the louder, "Jesus, Son of David, have mercy on me." Finally Jesus approaches the man and says to him, "What is it that you want of me?" The blind man replies, "Lord, open my eyes so that I may see."

This is my prayer during the times when I cannot see something clearly or do not know the solution to a certain situation.

Lord, open my eyes so that I may see.

I say it over and over during the day. Those empty moments—when I am walking or driving from one place to another or when I am just waiting for someone—give me the opportunity to strengthen my union with the Divine.

The mind is delicate and impressionable. We often think that we have strong minds, but we do not really understand how delicate they can be. One thing is certain: as one of my schoolteachers used to say, "Garbage in, garbage out." If we put garbage into our minds, we will only get garbage out of our minds. This is why our education systems are so important.

Education is designed to eliminate ignorance, thus assisting us in reaching our fulfillment. When you teach truth, you eliminate ignorance and do humanity an immeasurable service. When you teach partial truths and lies, you create ignorance.

Another friend of mine once said to me, "What you read today walks and talks with you tomorrow." If you go to a party and someone introduces a book to the discussion, chances are the person has just read or is reading that book. What we read affects us. We read stories of heroism with characters whose qualities we admire, and we try to apply these qualities to our own lives. On the other side of the equation, there are countless examples of people who have read tales of violence and destruction and then gone out and imitated those actions.

Personally I have never been a strong reader, but I do like to read. I read slowly and reflectively, trying to absorb what I am reading so that I can apply it to my life if it will be beneficial. This is why I choose carefully what I read.

Another aspect of our lives that can have a tremendous effect on us is music. Music can lift the spirit and make the spirit within us dance. It can inspire and motivate us. Yet when it is not used to focus us on things that are good and true, the things with which we wish to fill our lives, music can embitter us and enslave us to misery. Music has a powerful ability to direct our thoughts. So often we will hear a song early in the morning and we find ourselves humming, singing, or whistling that song throughout the day. Music directs our thoughts, but toward what? Does the music we listen to help us to focus on the things that are good, true, and honorable? Or does the music we listen to lead us away from our fulfillment and toward emptiness?

Our minds are precious instruments given to us by God to assist us on the path of fulfillment and happiness. When we fill our minds with ideas that contradict our purpose, we weaken ourselves unnecessarily. Human thought is powerful. When we use our thoughts to fix our direction and to outline our goals, amazing advances can be achieved.

Nothing influences your words and actions more than what you allow to occupy your mind.

CHAPTER 7

TRUTH AND FREEDOM

**If *freedom* is not the most misunderstood
word in any language today, it is second only
to *humility,* which is the key to freedom.**

WE have all heard many a teenager cry, "I want more freedom." But is it really freedom that these young people want? No. What they want is to be able to do whatever they want when they want. This is not true freedom.

Freedom is the ability to choose what is right. Thus, freedom in its purest form is found only in slavery— that is, we who are slaves to truth are truly free.

There are, of course, many different types of freedom. You are free to dine at the Waldorf but you cannot dine for free. So your freedom in this case is dependent on your financial situation. Political liberty is a freedom that belongs only to those fortunate enough to live in a country whose constitution affords such freedom. You have the freedom to choose your profession, but your choice is dependent on your academic abilities. These types of freedom are restricted; they are not absolute or complete. For by choosing to be a lawyer, you prevent yourself from being a doctor, and by choosing to buy a fast new car, you prevent yourself from spending that money in a hundred different ways.

Another type of freedom is the freedom to do as one ought. While an animal is a slave to its passions and sensuous desires, humans are equipped with the freedom to do what they ought or ought not to do. When we embrace this freedom, it allows reason to dominate over the passions in accord with a higher law.

But this type of freedom also allows us to choose otherwise. And the cost of exercising this freedom appropriately is often very high. For example, you make a computer error at your job in a bank, and you know that if the mistake is traced to you, you will lose your job. The only way that your boss can find out, however, is if you admit to the error. You possess the freedom of will to admit the mistake, but the cost of exercising such freedom may be your job. One who is a slave to truth would admit the error and thus surrender her position because of her just exercise of freedom. She realizes that her freedom is of much greater value than her job. This freedom of the will is very different from the freedom to do as one wishes.

The human being is a delicate composition of body and soul, an intertwining of the material and the immaterial. The material part of the human being (the body) is governed by one set of laws, while the immaterial parts (the intellect, will, soul) are governed by their own laws. An understanding of our free choice is essential not only to understanding what we are as human beings but also to understanding how we can move toward fulfillment, completion, and perfection.

Even a prisoner possesses some freedom to do as he wishes within the constraints of his imprisonment. And certainly we all enjoy the freedom to think whatever we choose. We are all entitled to our own opinions, but this does not make all opinions equal. For example, if it is your opinion that all opinions are equal while another person believes that all opinions are *not* equal, then based on your belief, you must admit that his opinion is equal to yours, even though it directly contradicts your own.

There are many types or degrees of freedom. The highest and the greatest of these is the freedom to choose what is right.

In the midst of this we are brought to the question that is as old as humanity. What is truth? We seek truth. The experiences of our lives unfold truth for us, and once we have discovered some element of truth, we either embrace it or try to ignore it. By embracing it we become a little truer and a little freer; by ignoring it we become slaves to a lesser reality, which often consists of pleasure, comfort, possessions, or pride.

JESUS AND TRUTH

**Jesus came to set humanity free. His ways are
truth and "the truth will set you free."**

In the times of ancient Israel the People of God
awaited the Messiah. Jesus was the Messiah sent to set
the children of God free. But when He arrived, the type
of freedom He proclaimed was not the freedom the
people wanted. They wanted a Messiah who would lead
them to political freedom. Our foolish pride was once
again not prepared to bow to the grand ways of God.

In this respect, nothing has changed in two thousand
years. Men and women still want freedom, and they
still choose the lesser forms of freedom: the freedom
that gives them power to take away other people's freedom; the freedom to do as they wish, when they wish,
how they wish. These are not aspects of true freedom. It
is like calling arsenic "chocolate" or liquid nitrogen
"cola." These behaviors set no one free but rather enslave those who dedicate their lives to them.

**Truth is the only thing worth living for and the
only thing worth dying for.**

If there is one thing that will give you freedom, it is
truth. When Jesus said, "The truth will set you free," He
was certainly referring to humanity's redemption. His
words do, however, have a practical application for our
lives today, and we can discover this application by asking, when we seek freedom, not "How can I achieve
greater autonomy and independence?" but rather "What
is truth?"

If as we move through each day and as we face decisions in our lives, we can ask this question and to some

degree answer it, we will be closer to gaining true freedom. However, knowledge of truth does not set a person free. In attaining a greater knowledge of truth, a person is called to respond in word and deed by abiding in that truth, and it is this abiding in truth that gives the person freedom. Finally, with this freedom come peace, joy, happiness, and a greater ability to love.

The truth, however, is not always something that just jumps out at us in every moment of the day. And sometimes in the larger decisions in our lives it can be very difficult to distinguish truth from falsehood.

From moment to moment we must learn to listen to the voice of conscience that whispers within us prior to our every word and deed. Listening to this voice is an acquired art; it is difficult and comes only with practice. To increase your ability to hear what your conscience is telling you, you must obey what it tells you. The more you obey that inner voice, the clearer it becomes. But be assured from the outset that the voice will make demands of you, will challenge you, and will ask you countless times a day to go against your lower animal instincts.

Nothing brings greater joy than abiding in truth, living by the law of God, and listening to the voice of conscience.

We need to acknowledge that the voice of truth and conscience is not necessarily the only voice you will hear. The voice of the evil spirit may also make its presence felt, particularly as you first begin to change. Be careful, be cautious, be discerning, but do not be afraid. Ask God, who is the author and source of truth and goodness, to be with you and protect you from deception. Pray openly and honestly, asking for the wisdom to be open to the spirit of truth, for the discernment to hear the truth of your conscience, and for the strength to live what you hear.

A general rule is that if you hear anything from within or from an external source that would bring harm to yourself or to anyone else, this is not the voice of truth.

Apart from this inner voice, there exist both natural and moral laws. People are created to live in harmony with God and with each other. To achieve this, each person must acquire a spirit of self-sacrifice. Greed does not create harmony, nor do hatred, gossip, slander, abuse, violence, and any number of other things that take place throughout our societies.

It is time to take a good look at the society in which we live and to ask ourselves what lies in store for a culture if it based on death, destruction, and abuse. These abominations are characteristic of our age. They lead not only to all sorts of problems within a culture but finally to the destruction of that culture. This has happened countless times throughout the ages, and it will happen again unless you and I make changes. Our society is headed for ruin not because God is going to send it to us but because we—you and I and our neighbors—are bringing destruction on ourselves.

Our society holds up lies to be honored. The teenage population of the Western world adores pop stars and movie stars, many of whom portray on and off the screen lifestyles that deny that the human being has a soul. Their lifestyles send out this message loud and clear: have fun, enjoy yourself, extract from life as much physical pleasure as you can, and amass as much wealth and possessions as possible in your lifetime. The one thing that is certain for us all is that we will die, yet most people live as if they were immortal.

What place have we given truth in our society? What place have we given truth in our lives? We all want freedom, yet we continue to shun the one thing that will bring us the freedom we desire: the *truth* will set you free.

What this world needs is a group of men and women who are prepared to sacrifice all the worldly pleasures and comforts in order to pursue truth. This is what the spiritual life is about. This is what the academic life is about; this is what the family life is about; this is what the political life is about; this is what the legal life is about; this is what the medical life is about; this is what *life* is about. Seeking, discovering, and living truth. Without men and women in society who are prepared to lead by example and make this their all-encompassing goal in life, our society is doomed. There is no future for any society that allows immorality and lies to be their leaders, goals, and heroes.

Religion, stated simply, is about how humanity relates to God. It is about tapping into the power of the Divine. In the Christian tradition we believe that through baptism we become one with God. We form a union with God. We are called to live in Him as He lives in us. Imagine that the love, truth, and wisdom of God are an umbrella. Through baptism we are brought underneath this umbrella. Insomuch as we live in truth, we live in God and remain under the umbrella. But when we live a lie, we step out from under the umbrella of God's love, truth, and wisdom. God does not stop loving us, but we have placed an obstacle between ourselves and God. We say no to God and truth and yes to something that is false and ultimately destructive.

Morality is about choices. It is about joy and misery, and in each moment the choice is ours. I know deep within me if something is wrong, even if I do not fully understand why it is wrong. For me to know that it is wrong is enough.

My obedience to what I know to be right brings me joy. My disobedience to what I know is right brings me misery.

It is not necessary for us to be told that some things are wrong. Countless cultures since the beginning of time bear testament to this fact. For example, most cultures have recognized that to kill an innocent person is wrong. In self-defense nature sometimes ordains it necessary to take the life of a perpetrator. Paul writes about the Gentiles who without being told of the law of God abide by it on many counts: "When Gentiles who have not the law do by nature what the law requires, they are a law to themselves, even though they do not have the law. They show that what the law requires is written on their hearts, while their conscience also bears witness" (Romans 2:15).

There are some things that were intrinsically engraved on the hearts of men and women at the moment of creation. One is that there exists a greater being than themselves, who is all-powerful and the source of every blessing. To love God is the vocation of every man and every woman. This vocation is fulfilled in practical terms by loving one's neighbor. These things we know always, even if we are unable to express them articulately or at all. They are engraved on our souls and on our hearts, and all happiness comes from abiding by them. You and I can ignore them, but we can never remove them. They are a part of us from now through eternity.

If we are to advance spiritually, we must place truth at the center of our hearts, minds, and souls. Of course this spiritual advancement means increasing our freedom, happiness, and our ability to love, although these in themselves are not our goal. Our goal is to reach the fulfillment for which we were created, to become what we were created to be. It is to live up to our role as sons and daughters of God.

How should the sons and daughters of God act? In truth and with love, because that is how God would act. God in His infinite wisdom sent His Son Jesus to the world to redeem humanity and to give us a model to live by. The Christian way of life is governed and lived by one question: what would Jesus do or say now? If we can answer that question and live the answer, then freedom is ours.

During His time on earth Jesus also said, "You will do all these things and much greater." We know the acts that He did and the love, the compassion, and the understanding He showed. He healed people, He fed people miraculously, He called people back to life from death. Is it possible for these things to be an everyday reality in our world today? Yes, absolutely. Why then are they not? Because we are liars. We lie. In little ways and in large ways, our lives are full of lying words and actions that separate us from God and prevent His power from flowing through us. He is the source of every miracle, yet He uses us so often to work miracles on earth. If we do not cooperate, then we are at a loss. In us Heaven and earth meet, yet we are capable of limiting the influence Heaven has in our lives. That is freedom. We are able to say no to the God who created us and sustains our life in every moment. There is no greater freedom. But if we exercise that freedom by turning our backs on God, then we enslave ourselves to the foolish pursuit of the types of freedom that are but ghosts of the freedom that sets us free, allowing our spirits to soar and achieve wondrous things.

To take the spiritual journey we must become slaves to truth. Listen to the voice of your conscience and act on what you hear. The voice will become clearer and clearer, and you will become free. Your life will become a dance for joy, and you will feel life's burdens being lifted from your shoulders. Your spirit will soar.

If you want happiness, freedom, and the ability to love and be loved from this moment on, you need to make a resolution: *stop lying.* Do not lie to yourself and do not lie to others. When you lie, you surrender your peace; you become uneasy because you have to watch everything you say. The first lie then demands another lie to support it, and so on.

If you discover yourself lying, *stop.* Apologize to the person to whom you are lying, especially if it is yourself. Then tell the truth. If you are embarrassed to apologize to whomever you are lying to, then you need to ask yourself what is more important: truth or lies? Freedom or slavery? Joy or misery? The other person will only respect you more if you tell the truth, and the world in a small way will be a better place. Next time that person is lying, he will recall your mistake and may change his ways. He in turn will affect another in a positive way. You will be setting not only yourself free but also your friend and whomever else he touches. Your telling the truth will be like a stone dropped in stagnant water. The stone produces a ripple, the first ripple another, the second ripple another, and so on until the ripples reach the opposite shore. But without the stone falling in the water, there will be no ripples and no positive change.

Your change is important not only for you but also for your neighbor, for your country, and for the world.

To discover truth you must be open to the truth. To the extent that you open yourself and struggle to live whatever truth you know, you will continue to have truth revealed to you.

Don't tell a lie—not a big lie, not a small lie, not a partial truth, not even a small fabrication— and the truth of the natural and the supernatural realms will be opened to you.

CHAPTER 8

A SPIRITUAL APPROACH TO THE EVERYDAY

The world has known many saints, many successful people, many happy people. They have attained and enjoyed their sanctity, success, and happiness one day at a time.

DESPITE the many miseries that we are aware of in the world, it really is a world of joy and plenty. Sometimes we are not able to see this because of humanity's greed and selfishness, but in the heroism of certain individuals it comes shining through every day.

**If you watch carefully, you will catch a glimpse
of heroism even in people in whom you least
expect to find a hero.**

Much of what I have said in this book is aimed at
showing how the supernatural is the supreme aspect of
our lives because it stretches into eternity. In this chapter, however, I would like to focus on the natural elements of our human existence and try to show how the
message applies to them as well.

Just because we have begun to focus on the supernatural does not mean that we should neglect the natural.
While on this earth the spirit within us, our soul,
makes its home in our body. Therefore, while on this
earth the natural supports the supernatural element in
each person.

By an infinite grace that we perhaps will never understand, God has given us life as men and women not
only with bodies and instincts like the animals but also
with souls assisted by the powers of intellect and will.
He has made us in His image and placed us on the earth
to be "fruitful and multiply." The main determinant of
this "fruitfulness" is the enthusiasm with which we develop the image of God within us. Created in the image
of God, we were given superabundant gifts. God then
crowned us with the gift of freedom. This freedom
means that while God created us in His image, it is up
to us to sustain ourselves in the image of God and, even
more, to grow in that image. God has given us the necessary gifts to remain and grow in His image, but His
gift of freedom means that He will not intervene and
impose this sustenance or growth on us.

**Your fruitfulness on this earth is measured in
the eyes of God by one thing alone: to what
extent have you struggled to grow in the image
of God?**

On this earth we have many concerns. Some of them
we should pay attention to, while others are to be re-
nounced. The world in which we live often reflects the
splendor of the Divine, yet there are those occasions
when we prevent the wonder of God from being displayed. Despite the setbacks this life can bring and despite the problems that fill our world, it is a wonderful
place and is to be loved and cherished by us all, for it
was made by God and is therefore good.

**To despise the world is not the attitude of Christ.
It is the way man acts that makes the world the
way it is. When man acts like an animal, his ways
deserve to be despised by all intelligent beings.
When man, who was created in the image of God,
acts like God, the splendor and wonder of His
Kingdom come alive here on this earth.**

Our concerns are God and His ways, family, friendship, work, and leisure. These intertwine with culture
and understanding to form the richness of life. Each of
these areas must have a place in our everyday lives.
One should not be neglected completely in order to fulfill another.

Our priorities can be put in an order that promises
balance and fulfillment for each of us:

God and His ways
Family

Friends

Work

Leisure

Many people today have made their careers and work the most important aspect of their lives. They have distorted the natural order and surrendered to a life of disorder. This leads them to be imbalanced, unfulfilled, and eventually unhappy.

Like anything worth achieving in our lives, this balance and order come only by making an effort. Some people randomly try to juggle all the elements of their lives without assigning a priority to each of them, and then they wonder constantly whether or not they are achieving the balance and order they sense they are capable of. They are not.

To achieve this order with any consistency requires a systematic approach. It requires a plan, a pattern, or a schedule. For most of us, a schedule was something that we learned to draw up in high school or in some study-skills program in order to help us manage our time. And most of us never lived up to the schedule we came up with. But the important thing now is that we recognize that our days are made up of only so many hours and that there are an infinite number of ways to spend that limited time. Unless we consciously make a decision about how we will use each day, we will waste time doing unnecessary things and put off activities that are vital if we are to experience fulfillment and happiness.

When I woke up this morning, I knew that the most important thing for me to do today was to pray. Yet when I woke up I did not consciously have to plan when I would pray today. This is because before I went to bed last night I decided that this morning when I woke up, I would shower, eat my breakfast, and then spend time in prayer before allowing the day's activities to swallow me up. For me it is important to pray early in the day. Prayer is the most important activity of my day so I must give it top priority. This only makes sense, but I still need a plan or schedule to ensure that I act on this priority.

At this point let me make one point very clear: you will never live up to your schedule perfectly. In fact, if you do, then there is not enough on it. The purpose of the schedule is not to enslave us but to motivate us and give us the direction and balance necessary to live happy, fulfilled lives. The schedule is for us; we are not for the schedule. The schedule is a tool. The worker controls the tool; the tool does not control the worker. And like all tools, the use of a schedule also requires the use of common sense. For example, if a friend calls you to go have coffee because she needs to talk, but your schedule says that you should spend this time studying, your Christian duty to love obviously overrules your resolution to stick to your schedule.

We use schedules to help bring the most out of ourselves, but schedules are not laws.

Our time is a gift. It is limited and valuable. It is to be used in fruitful endeavors and not to be wasted. From very early in my life I was taught this truth by my parents. And throughout my life the lesson has been reinforced by the inspirational examples of countless people. Only recently my father sent me a letter with the following story in it. It came to me at a time when I really needed to reassess how I was using my time. This story reminded me that each day we have a marvelous opportunity to achieve something.

> If you had a bank that credited your account each morning with $86,400, that carried over no balance from day to day, that allowed you to keep no cash in your account, and that every evening canceled whatever part of the amount you had failed to use during the day, what would you do?
>
> Well, you have such a bank. Its name is Time. Every morning it credits you with 86,400 seconds. Every night it writes off as lost whatever of this you have failed to invest to good purpose. It carries over no balances. It allows no overdrafts.
>
> Each day it opens a new account with you. Each night it burns the records of the day. If you fail to use the day's deposits, the loss is yours. There is no going back. There is no drawing against "tomorrow." You must live in the present on today's deposits.
>
> Invest it so as to get from it the utmost in health, happiness, and success! And don't forget to give God some of this time!

In order to use our time wisely, we need to employ some method such as a plan or a schedule to assist us.

If you want to use your day well, assess your priorities, write them down in order, and allocate the necessary time to each of them from the first priority on down until your days are full enough to be fulfilling but not so full as to be damaging.

Most of the ideas in this chapter have not come to
me by any supernatural means. This does not make
them worthless or any less true than the ideas that I
have presented in the preceding chapters. Our goal is to
grow to be better people, to grow in the image of God
and in the likeness of Christ. The ideas in this chapter
have been shared with me by hundreds of people
throughout my life. They are not new and they are not
spectacular, but they are necessary. Without them I
could not have walked the path I have walked and am
walking.

Just as we look back on the accomplishments and
failures of previous generations, the generations to come
will look back on the time in which you and I live.
These are our days, given to us as a gift, entrusted to us
as an opportunity for sanctity, success, and happiness.

FOOD, EXERCISE, AND SLEEP

**To experience any type of success in the spiri-
tual life, you must always remember that while
we inhabit this earth, our bodies are the homes
of our souls and therefore should be respected
and maintained in fitness and health.**

During my late teenage years I used to think that eating and sleeping were a waste of time. My mother was
always telling me to eat more slowly and sleep more.
As I look back, I can see clearly that the unhappiness I
have experienced because of my own actions has been
caused because I have not been concerned with my
whole person. At times I neglected my very self to

achieve some goal that already, in the space of only a few years, has become insignificant.

I now realize that regular sleep and a healthy diet are important components in my life and that exercise enhances my performance and everything else I do, including my prayer life.

—◦◦◦—

As I mentioned earlier, I met a priest shortly after I began hearing the voice of God. He is a wonderful man full of humor and energy for life. I would spend time speaking with him about the struggles I was having as I tried to live out the message. On many occasions I would come to him, and he could tell I was tired or had not had enough sleep. He would say to me, "Matthew, the first step toward your becoming a saint is for you to get eight hours of sleep every night." And in one of the messages I have received, God the Father speaks about waking up and going to bed at the same time each day. He showed me that by setting these two times in your day, you create order in your life.

Order breeds efficiency.

In the Bible we read that God rewards the just man with the sleep of the righteous. I so often meet people who think that to go without sleep is a saintly act. In college it is common to hear people boasting about staying up all night working on a paper, as if this were an act of heroism worthy of admiration. Instead, it merely shows that they lack the order and discipline necessary to get the work done in the hours that God created for work. I have spent many a night working myself. But I have learned that without sleep, or without enough sleep, you cannot be effective in completing your daily tasks.

In some cases God asks us for heroism by giving us a task or mission that requires us to give up sleep. In cases where this is part of the plan held by God, it is God who gives the grace to fulfill the task heroically. This is the difference between necessary and unnecessary heroism.

Sleeping at the same time each night offers the most effective rest, and this rest time is important for you not only physically but also spiritually. When we sleep, we surrender our whole being to God for Him to renew, refresh, and strengthen. Before going to sleep at night, I take just a few seconds to entrust myself to His loving protection. I ask Him to soften my heart, to increase my receptivity of His grace, and to increase my ability to love throughout the day.

One of our most amazing faculties is the ability to dream. We do not quite know why we dream or what influence or meaning dreams have for human existence, but we know that this faculty is powerful. While we sleep, we are able, through the power of our imagination, to experience events as if they were actually happening. We can feel joy and fear, pain and pleasure, sorrow and exhilaration. In every age men and women of all cultures have believed in the power of dreams, though few have understood them. Knowing how important they are, we have developed our ability to daydream, to imagine how we would like the future to unfold. In the Bible there are countless accounts of dreams being God's medium to communicate with people. We read in the early chapters of Matthew's gospel how God spoke to Joseph in a series of dreams that led and directed him, encouraging him to have trust and courage and to abandon his fears. Perhaps dreams are God's forgotten language. Dreaming is, no doubt, part of the human experience for reasons that the providence of God will unfold in time.

———⁓⁓⁓———

Eating is as important as sleeping. Eat often and well but in moderation and never to the point of gluttony. Fasting is a valuable means to discipline, a suitable expression of love, and an indispensable spiritual tool, but it can easily lead a soul to the pride of the Pharisees.

———⁓⁓⁓———

Exercise brings oxygen to the brain and has a tremendous ability to clear the mind of all useless anxiety. It increases our ability to concentrate and renews and refreshes our bodies. When practiced regularly and consistently, exercise leads a person to be more relaxed and more effective in every aspect of life.

Twenty minutes a day of exercise will make you feel like a new person in ten days.

This need for regular exercise is no supernatural revelation. But it nonetheless truthfully describes the way we are made. If we desire to be fully alive and to strive for our fulfillment and sanctity, we must pay due attention to every area of our lives and of our persons.

Be kind to yourself. Eat, sleep, and exercise.

WORK

"In the beginning God created Heaven and earth. . . . God then said, 'Let us make man in our own image,'

... and then the Lord God took the man and put him in his garden of delight to cultivate and tend it" (Genesis 1:1, 26; 2:15). The original occupation of man was to tend and cultivate the garden. God created man to work.

We were created to work and we have a serious obligation to work hard and well, because our time on earth is a gift entrusted to us by God. When we pass from this life, we will be called to make account of how we have used our time.

Our work can take many forms; for many people, for example, academic studies constitute their full-time occupation. But whatever our work, it provides opportunities for us to grow in holiness, to build friendships, and to spread the faith. In addition to our work, we all as Christians have an obligation to study our faith in order to grow in our understanding of God and His ways and so that we can share and defend our faith.

Even while modern attitudes toward work continue to be overwhelmingly negative, God is calling us to approach the workplace cheerfully and creatively, allowing our words and actions to reflect the gospel message.

The field is the world, the harvest is great, and we are being called by Our Father, the Lord of the harvest, to be His laborers and do His work wherever in the world we find ourselves.

As modern philosophies continue to separate the things of our everyday lives from matters of faith, our Christian witness in the workplace is of greater value and importance than ever. We need to show people that all the events of our lives, particularly our work, are compatible with our faith. In fact, our work only takes on its true meaning and value when united to our Christian beliefs.

Modern philosophies and ideas have built a wall between the everyday happenings of our lives and our faith. The result is the misguided belief that to be holy one needs to run away from the world.

On getting up one morning, a man asked himself, "Why do I go to work?" The reply he gave himself was "To earn money so I can support myself and my family." For a Christian, however, there is much more.

As Christians, our work is something we undertake as a service to society. It also provides the means for our daily sanctification and an ideal opportunity to offer a Christian example and through friendship to gather others into the company of Christ, as well as the fulfillment of our temporal needs and those of our family.

Every event in our lives is an opportunity to be holy. For most of us, our work absorbs the majority of the hours in the day, so the ideal of a modern apostle must be to turn every hour of work into an hour of prayer. This is achieved by offering each hour to God as a prayer for a special intention or particular friend, by paying attention to the detail of our work, and by making good use of our time.

The workplace can also be fertile ground in which we can sow the seed of God's word. Spending a large proportion of our days at work, we can be presented with many opportunities to build friendships and gain respect for the Christian life. These friendships can become the vehicle for us to spread the faith within the workplace.

Nobody who loves Christ and is capable of being the best at his or her given profession has any excuse for not being the best.

I am told that you want to follow Christ but that your work is sloppy and thoughtless. How disappointing this is to our God, who wants us to excel, who wants our best, who wants our all. As Christians we need to work well.

The starting point of working well is being attentive to detail. Little things are the most important because they make up the great things. Little by little. Not many things, just things done well. To be Christian is to be like Christ, and they said of Jesus, "He has done all things well." Could the same be said of you and me?

Often after watching an athlete excel at a sporting event or after seeing someone excel in any given field, I think to myself, "I wonder if they believe in God, and if not, imagine what they could do if they united their efforts with God, the author of excellence." There are so many people who are working unceasingly with their whole attention focused on the fulfillment of selfish ambitions and desires. How much more important it is for us who love God to work hard in all areas of our lives with our attention firmly fixed on our one and only ambition: Christ's reign on earth.

As a result of original sin, man has a tendency to take the path of least effort. This means that we must constantly struggle against laziness. Jesus said, "If any man wishes to come my way, let him renounce himself, take up his cross, and come and follow me" (Luke 9:23). The road that leads to Heaven is narrow, and the journey is a constant struggle.

Our hearts desire the good; however, "the spirit is willing but the flesh is weak" (Matthew 26:41). Or as

Saint Paul wrote, "the good that I would, I do not. The evil that I would not, it is that which I do." (Romans 7:19).

This struggle is the result of the disorder within us. When our first parents fell, the order with which God created them was replaced by the disorder that we now find ourselves forever trying to overcome. Our laziness, our desire to seek the easy road, to avoid duties, and to have comfort and pleasure must always be combated by our attempts to restore the order to our lives that was lost in the fall.

In our work the best way we can do this is by making a plan for each day. By spending a few moments each morning looking at what tasks you have to do, assessing their priority, and then allocating your time accordingly, you will move through your days with a clearer head and a better sense of direction.

If we don't, we tend to spend time talking to people or shuffling papers; we let ourselves be consumed by distractions until the important things pile up to the point that we become distressed and inefficient.

I don't think that we ever fully recognize the effect we have on the people around us. After prayer, our words and actions are the primary tool we have for spreading the faith, regardless of the environment. This is particularly true in the workplace.

Our work should be done well, with honesty and integrity. When we complete a task, it should be obvious that we have approached our work with attention to detail. Our relations with people in the workplace should always uphold the dignity of the other person. As sons and daughters of God, we should each strive for excellence in our particular occupation.

Above and beyond our duties in and around the workplace, we should offer the hand of friendship to those the Lord places in our path. A poem I recall from my childhood reads, "Life is mostly bubbles and froth, but two things stand in stone: kindness in others' troubles, and courage in our own." The boat of friendship can be enough to carry someone across the troubled waters to our greatest Friend, met through a life of prayer. The workplace is an opportunity to offer others that boat of friendship.

STUDY

How many of us have written up a schedule and never lived up to it? We should try to stick to our schedule and certainly make every attempt to avoid fruitless distractions. However, we must be careful that our schedule does not create within us an inflexible attitude that leads to a lack of charity and a single-mindedness that makes us unable to deal creatively with unexpected circumstances.

If anything, this is of greater importance for those whose full-time occupation is currently to be a student. To schedule our study and to stick to this schedule faithfully is important. Attention to the detail of the schedule is important, because in love all the little things are important. When we set to work on our studies, we should try to ensure that there are not too many distractions around. Phones, doorbells, friends, stereos, refrigerators, and televisions can all lead us away from our primary focus—learning.

Let us approach our work one hour at a time. Do it, do it well, every last minute, offering it to God for your aunt who isn't well, for that friend you are trying to bring closer to God, for the Church, for the holy souls in purgatory, or for that special intention of your own. The value of this hour placed in this perspective is enormous.

A handy tool can be to have a holy picture, or a crucifix, or just a cross where you work. Then when you look up from your work and see Saint Joseph there, ask him to intercede and obtain for you a noble attitude toward your work. Or if you look up and see Mary there beside you in your work, ask her to comfort you in the long hours of the day. Or when the load seems heavy, look up and see Jesus on the cross before you, then go back to work resolved to struggle. How little we have to go through by comparison.

There are obstacles to our work, and there are ways and means of overcoming them. We must make use of all the means available to us.

Regardless of what it is that occupies the hours of our day, God wants us to take time out to spend exclusively with Him. Balancing our work and our prayer time can be difficult, particularly with family commitments, but this balance is of paramount importance if we are to grow.

—◦◦◦—

The abbot of a monastery once was very concerned about a young monk's inability to grasp a practical understanding of the order's motto. The motto was "Work and pray."

The abbot prayed for months for the young monk and did everything in his power to explain and demonstrate the richness of the motto to him. And still the young monk was unable to see the hidden meaning of the motto, and his life as a result was full of disorder.

Weeks and months went by, and finally the abbot decided to take the young monk on an outing, spending some time with him in a different environment. He hoped that this would provide the opportunity to share with the young man how the motto had enriched his life at the monastery and assisted him in developing in the image of Christ, as well as how it had helped him to perfect various imperfections in his character.

The abbot asked the young monk if he would like to go rowing on the lake, and the young monk agreed. The following day they left the monastery before dawn, and soon they found themselves at the edge of the lake. They took the small rowboat to the edge of the water, and as they climbed in, the abbot said, "I'll row to the other side, and then you can row back for us." The young monk agreed, and the abbot began to row but only with one oar. He rowed and he rowed with the one oar, while they went around and around in a circle. The young monk sat in the boat saying nothing for a while, but finally, after they had gone around in a circle a few more times and as the sun began to come up, his impatience got the better of him and he said to the abbot, "You know, if you don't row with both oars we're never going to get anywhere." The abbot just smiled and looked the young man straight in the eye and replied, "Yes, you are right. Work and pray." The abbot had made his point, and the young man finally understood.

—◦◦◦—

Saint Paul wrote, "Pray constantly." It is clear that all of us cannot go into our churches all day long and pray. Furthermore, our need to sleep and eat prevents us from praying around the clock. God did not equip us to do this, but He did create us to pray constantly. What is Paul saying to us? Could it be that he is encouraging us to do something very practical in our Christian lives?

Every honest human activity is compatible with our faith and can be transformed into prayer. On numerous occasions I have expressed this idea to people, often to students, and they are quick to ask, "How?"

Suppose you are a student. Every day, every year, you read many pages of books and write many, many pages of notes. You spend much of your time and energy fulfilling your duties as a student. Are your efforts worthless in the sight of God? Have they no value in your journey toward salvation? Everything we do every day, as long as it is good and honest, has a value in the eyes of God. Indeed, every page you read or write has a value in the eyes of God and can assist in your salvation and the salvation of others.

However, it is important and will benefit your relationship with God enormously if you are aware of this in each of moment of the day. So from now on, take a pencil when you are studying, and at the top of each page you read and each page you write, put the initials of someone you know who needs your prayers. Then offer the work on that page to God as a prayer for that person. Similarly, if you are a doctor, offer the time you spend with each patient as a prayer for a person or a special intention. Likewise, if you are a milkman, offer each bottle of milk you deliver as a prayer. Perhaps you have a watch that chimes on the hour; each time it chimes, offer the next hour of your work to God as a prayer for a particular intention. Regardless of what our occupation is, our work can be and should be transformed into prayer. This is the real challenge that presents itself to us in the hours of our work.

This idea can also be applied to every aspect of family life and domestic living. For example, when you wash the dishes, offer the task as a prayer for someone who needs it; when you wash the car, offer the task as a prayer for a particular intention; when the baby wakes at three o'clock in the morning and you have to get out of a warm bed to feed him, offer the discomfort as a prayer for the child. Thus, every honest human activity is compatible with our faith and can be transformed into prayer.

When we begin to offer the events of our days one by one to God, we will grow in the awareness of God's presence, and we will begin to appreciate what Paul meant when he wrote, "Pray constantly."

WHO SHOULD STUDY THE FAITH?

The ultimate aim of everything we do in this life should be to love God. Clearly, you cannot love someone you do not know. Jesus is alive in His Church, and all His beauty and splendor are reflected in the Church's teachings.

In these times the Church is in desperate need of a cultural wave of study—men and women who seriously set out to grow in understanding of the Church's stance on different issues, people who are not led by blind faith but who use the resource of their God-given intellect to discover as much as they can about God. The basis of this study must be two questions that we should keep forever in our minds and hearts and on our lips: what does the Church teach? And why does the Church teach what she teaches?

It is important that the Catholic truths be sustained, maintained, and preserved through these times of confusion. The only way to achieve this is for people to live them. We cannot live something we do not know. We are all being called to study our faith in some way so as to assist in the defense of these truths by our example.

So many people have never read a catechism. Knowledge of the teachings of our faith clears the mind and conscience and removes confusion. Study the articles of our faith just one hour a week, or fifteen minutes a day; these small parcels of time will in the end make the difference.

WE MUST ANSWER FOR EACH HOUR

Morally we have a duty to give a fair day's work in return for a fair day's pay. For the Christian, however, the value of an hour's work far surpasses the hourly wage. Time is a gift well used by the wise. Will we hear our Lord calling to us, "Well done, good and faithful servant," when the day is done?

Very often God seems very far removed from us because we haven't learned to recognize His presence in our daily lives. When we recognize that He is with us in our work, accompanying us, assisting us, watching over us, this inspires us to work even harder.

How hard Joseph would have worked in the workshop knowing that our Lord was observing him. What attention to detail he would have exercised. How fine his work as a carpenter would have been.

—◆◆—

We are sons and daughters of God; we must work hard professionally, and we must also work hard in our Father's field. To do the latter we must study our faith and pray for those we are trying to bring closer to God. Every time we offer an hour of work and study as a prayer for some particular person, the smile of God's grace will shine especially on that person.

FAMILY

The future of the world will be determined by how we understand and approach family life.

The importance of the role the family plays in relation to the development or deterioration of society cannot be overstated. The family is the cornerstone of society. It is the embryo of the future.

If we take a glance at the history of the world, one of the signs of a society headed for peril is the deterioration of family life and values. In our own society the traditional family unit is threatened on many levels, and it is becoming more and more common to find single parents raising children. Sometimes change is good, but not when it goes against nature. If the problems of society seem overwhelming, so too do the problems of our own individual family situations.

Family life is a rich and rewarding, and sometimes a difficult experience. It often seems that the very people whom we should love most are those we have the most difficulty loving. One of the main reasons is that we judge too much. We know the people in our families. We know their faults, their failings, their weaknesses, and their pasts. It is hard sometimes to see the good in people when it is so easy to remember the bad.

But when we find ourselves in this situation, we need to remind ourselves that we inherit many of our virtues and vices from our families. We pick up both little and large ways of doing and saying things. In many ways we are mirrors for each other. Chances are the virtues that you see in another person that you admire are qualities that you possess or are trying to acquire. The same is true when you find vices or faults in a person's character; chances are you also have those faults. Often we become critical and judgmental instead of recognizing that we all have faults and accepting where each of us is in the battle to overcome them.

It seems the very ability we most desire to exercise in our own lives is the ability we want to deny the people we love: freedom. It is one of God's greatest gifts to humanity—the freedom to walk with God or the freedom to walk away from God; the ability to choose in a hundred different ways everyday.

We always seem to be ready to take this special gift away from those we love. So often we look at family members and wish that they would do things more the way we do them. Perhaps this is not the way we should look at it. We are, of course, convinced that the way we do things would be better for them or is the way of truth. We may well be right. We may have found the way of truth and fulfillment, and perhaps we only desire the good of the other person. But our approach is often flawed.

If we could, perhaps we would take away their freedom and lead them to do what we know would be best for them. But the problem is that then it would do them no good at all. They have to want it for themselves.

Say, for example, you have discovered the importance of a relationship with God, but one of your children has not and refuses even to discuss the topic. If you could, you would perhaps take her freedom away and let her experience a little of what you have experienced. Fortunately you cannot take away her freedom; this would be like marrying her to a young man she neither knows nor cares about, even though he may be a wonderful young man.

Within our families many different situations arise. We cannot solve all the problems for the people we love. We can help to smooth the path that they must walk, but we cannot walk the path for them. We cannot protect them from pain. We cannot change them, and we should not try. There is only one thing we can do, and that is to love. Our love for so many people in our lives is clear as crystal in our minds but difficult to see sometimes in our actions. Love is selfless, yet often our expressions of care and concern for those around us are mixed with selfish ambitions.

Our happiness and fulfillment, and our effectiveness at leading others to their happiness and fulfillment, are dependent on our ability to unite ourselves with God and to speak, think, and act as God Himself does. We are called to love the other members of our family. So perhaps we should ask the question, "How does God love?" He loves always with purity of intention. He loves for the sake of loving.

We can learn a little more here from the sun. The sun is always doing the same thing. The sun shines. It dances in the sky all day long. The sun shines all day long here in America, and while it is nighttime here, it shines all day long in Australia.

Now, sometimes clouds will get in the way of the sun, but the sun keeps shining. The sun doesn't try to move the clouds. It just shines. The sun shines, and shines, and shines, just as God loves, and loves, and loves.

With our families we are called to love as the sun shines. Sometimes clouds will get in the way. It is not our job to move the clouds. Our job is to shine.

The sun allows the clouds to block its rays just as God allows us to block His love. When we put up barriers to God's love, He doesn't all of a sudden take away our freedom and force His love and ways on us. No, He loves patiently and waits for clearer skies.

God allows. His allowance is one of His attributes that often leaves us astounded. But in understanding that love must be a free choice, we also come to see how essential this allowance is to the nature of God.

Our motivation for love, like so many other things in our lives, is often based on the results it will bring. So many activities in our world that should be fruitful and meaningful in themselves, we see only as a means to an end, as stepping-stones. Many go to college only so they can get a better job, for instance. Often we love only in the hope of changing people. Indeed, our love *will* inevitably change people, but we should not love *in order* to change people.

Within families we also tend to develop an inability to let people change or to believe and accept that some- one has changed.

Be assured of this: when you do decide to change and set out along that path, many of the people around you will not like it. Merely by changing, your presence will challenge them to change.

We don't like people to change, because their wit- ness to change challenges us to change. And so in our families, we often become each other's worst enemies in the struggle to change and grow.

For example, when people are trying to change, they are trying to leave their past behind for a better and brighter future. In order for them to achieve this, they must keep their focus fixed on the change they wish to achieve. Often, however, we become uncomfortable when we see a family member changing, because this change reminds us of our own need to change. We try to justify or defend ourselves, even though the person changing is not attacking us.

We often resort to reminding the person who is try- ing to change of his mistakes in the past. Over and over again we remind that person of things he said or did somewhere along the way. Through this useless com- parison, we convince ourselves that we are not really so bad after all. But in doing so, we are missing the one distinguishing point: the other person is now trying to change and grow, and we are not.

The worst part of all is that by bringing up the person's past over and over, we take that person's mind off the changes he is trying to make in his life and place it back on the things he is trying to eliminate. Thus, we make it much harder for this person to change.

Placed together on this earth in families, we are meant to lead each other toward our common goal. We are meant to help each other love God and grow to fulfillment. When we do not share the same goal or when we are lukewarm in these ambitions, we tend to prevent those around us from achieving their potential.

Encouragement is what family life is about. We are all on the same journey, and more often than not we just need a little encouragement from the people we love.

LIFE

Whatever you do to another you do to yourself.

Love expresses itself in respect for and understanding of life. Love is life giving. In these times in which we live, humanity has failed to grasp the most elementary spiritual principle and Christian premise: however we treat other people, we treat ourselves. Now, this is not just some idea designed to make us feel guilty and to force us to treat each other with kindness and care. It is, in fact, a mystical reality.

Our inability to respect each other points to many flaws in our understanding of ourselves as human beings. It shows clearly that we do not fully understand that we as human beings are a composition of body and soul and that the soul is eternal and has an infinite value.

Our failure to treat each other with respect also shows how little we understand God as the living God and the life-giving God. All life comes from God.

So often in our homes we see a tiny ant that could never cause harm, and our first reaction is to kill it. Why? Do we actually feel threatened? In our minds we have formed the idea that the ant does not belong in the house. It is not convenient, so we kill it.

This may seem like a small example, but the cumulative effects of such attitudes are crippling to humanity.

So often we sit down at a table in a restaurant and on the table is a fresh flower. Now, a flower can be loved and appreciated on many different levels. You may look at a flower and see that it is beautiful and pleasing and love it for that. Or you may look at the flower and recognize that the same life force that sustains the life of the flower sustains your own life. Then your observance will have assisted you to grow in love of the flower and of life. God sustains the life of the flower just as He sustains your life. Furthermore you may look at the flower, see that it is beautiful and pleasing, and recognize that its beauty and splendor as part of creation are only a dim reflection of the God who created it. This will leave you in love with the flower, in love with life, and in love with God.

When was the last time you really appreciated the beauty and wonder of a flower? If we could appreciate the smaller aspects of creation like flowers, how much more would we appreciate the next person we meet?

Respect for life must be developed at every level. Our inability to see life as being sacred has led us to apply the disposable attitude of the nineties even to life itself. If a person is old or terminally ill or if a child is unwanted, we kill him or her. At the same time we speak out against the injustice of murder and violence within our society. Our streets are not safe because we promote disrespect for life.

It will never be safe to walk down the street until we reassess our attitudes toward life. Until life within the womb of a mother is safe, life outside the womb, in this world of ours, will never be safe.

Abortion is the ultimate sign that humanity has failed to understand that life is precious and sacred and that the human person is made up of body and soul.

If someone took to the streets of New York City today with an automatic weapon and killed four thousand people, it would make the front pages of every newspaper in the world.

Every day of the year four thousand abortions are committed in America. Four thousand human beings are killed. Four thousand innocent souls are sent prematurely into eternity because their life, which is sacred, is inconvenient. Hardly a word is spoken of these little ones.

Abortion not only kills an unborn child, it also breeds a mentality that life is disposable. It breeds a mentality that if it is inconvenient, kill it. What happens if one day you become inconvenient to someone?

Once upon a time America was a great country because it stood for, and represented, all that was good and true. America will again be a great country when it once more begins to stand up for what is good and true. The prosperity of any nation depends upon this.

In the past four years I have traveled to more countries than I ever imagined I would in my life. America stands above them all as a nation with tremendous potential to influence the world in a positive way. My heart hopes and waits for the day when the people and the leaders of this nation decide individually to exercise their influence and live, defend, and proclaim all that is good and true.

As a Christian I believe that if I wrong you, I wrong myself because we are one body. We must live together in harmony so that we can work together to make our family, our church, our city and state, our country and world the places and communities God designed them to be. He has entrusted them to us. We can destroy or enrich them. But be assured, if we destroy them we will be destroying ourselves, and if we enrich them we will enrich ourselves.

The future of our families, our countries, our church, and our world stand in peril unless wiser men and women with a respect and understanding of the mystery of life are forthcoming.

Take a little time each day to reflect on the mystery and wonder of life—first in nature, then in animals, and finally in people, especially yourself. By doing so your behavior toward all living things will change. You will learn to love all of them more. And you will learn to love yourself much more deeply.

—◠◠◠—

There are many factors that contribute to a healthy, happy, holy life. It is a matter of balancing the material and the spiritual. It is important to enjoy the material from the perspective of the spiritual. The journey is about allowing the real you to emerge, the you that is one with Christ. In struggling to perfect ourselves, we must pay due attention not only to the areas pertaining to the spirit but also to the matters pertaining to our everyday material existence. Jesus Christ came to save the whole person; the task of attaining sanctity, then, involves the whole person.

CHAPTER 9

THE IDEAL

There is nothing more attractive than holiness.

AN OPPORTUNITY

During these times, which strike many as being extraordinary, God's call is the same as always, and indeed God is too. So if changes for the better are to occur, what we need now more than ever are saints. Yes, saints—men and women who respond lovingly and wholeheartedly to God's call. You and I, my brothers and sisters, are all individually and uniquely being called to become saints.

Why is it that as I write these words about the high ideals of holy lives—and the only ideal of a Christian life—I sense that many will feel uneasy as they read them?

This uneasiness, I believe, witnesses to the fact that sanctity is misunderstood and that the ideal of a Christian life has been eroded by a common kind of compromise founded mostly in self-justification. Self-justification manifests itself in the many faithless philosophies of these modern times. In fact, in a time when the world is most in need of saints, the people of the world are least aware of what is involved in living a saintly life.

Clearly every Christian's goal in this life should be to conquer the pirates and overcome the storms so as someday to safely reach the port of Heaven. A saint is precisely that: someone who reaches Heaven. And so sanctity should be our goal. Yet so many of us wander through life without this direction, forgetting our purpose or never discovering it.

The world portrays a saint as someone who is a social misfit, who never smiles, and who does not know how to enjoy himself or herself. People think that holiness is like a gem lost in a haystack. Others believe that holiness is about running away and leaving the world. Some think that to be holy one must be constantly on one's knees praying.

These are all the unnatural and unattractive images that the world has put forth of a person trying to attain holiness.

But the truth is that there is nothing more attractive than holiness. Nothing is more attractive than virtue.

Holiness is about imitating Christ; it is about loving God. Holiness is an opportunity. Every moment of our lives, each person who enters our lives, every event or circumstance in our lives are opportunities to be holy. The sanctity or holiness of an individual is measured by how lovingly that person grasps the present moment for God, responding as Christ Himself would to the challenges that this moment presents. Thus, our humble and docile cooperation with the will of God, manifested in the way we respond to the people and events of our lives, determines our holiness.

God calls every man and every woman without exception, regardless of their occupation, position in the world, age, or vocation; from each and every single one of us He expects love. And He expects that love to be consistent and persevering.

God expects this love to express itself in two ways: first, in an intimate friendship with Jesus, and second, in our words and actions, by grasping each hour of our days and giving them all to God through doing His will, which is that we imitate Christ.

It is only through an intimate relationship with Jesus that we are able to achieve the latter. Through this friendship we come to know Jesus, who is true God and true man. You cannot love and imitate someone you do not know, and if our place in Heaven, our sanctity, is dependent on our love of God, it is clear that we must come to know God.

Our relationship with Christ is founded, just as any genuine friendship in this world is founded, on a knowledge of the other person through conversation. These conversations lead to an understanding that in turn increases our ability to communicate. And this communication results in an ever-deepening friendship.

It is conversation with Christ that nurtures sanctity. This conversation can take many forms, and just as a human relationship can develop to the stage where sometimes there is no need for discussion, at times just to be in the presence of Christ with our attention focused on Him is enough.

It is through prayer that we become friends with Christ, and it is this time spent in prayer that prepares us to grasp each moment of the day for God.

Sanctity is not only about giving each moment of our lives to God but about doing so consistently and perseveringly. Prayer prepares our hearts and minds to respond lovingly to the holy desires the Spirit places in our souls during the other moments of the day.

Quite simply, if our life of prayer is inconsistent, our ability to do or know God's will throughout the day will have the same inconsistency. And as a result, our love of God will be unnecessarily limited and inconsistent. These are not qualities commonly found in the lives of the saints. Rather, the saints are well known for their consistent and fervent lives of prayer, which flowed into a wonderful fidelity to the will of God, that manifested itself in their imitation of Christ in the daily activities of their lives.

Not only are they well known for these, but they are saints because the fragments of their lives are sewn together by these very characteristics. Prayer is the red carpet along which a saint walks; it is the key to sanctity.

THIS IS THE WILL OF GOD: THAT YOU BE SAINTS

In every decision that lies before us, one concern must predominate, and that is the will of God. Throughout the day, and at those special times each day when we come before the tabernacle, we must constantly be asking, "Lord, what is it that you want of me now?" He will place the answer in our hearts if we are prepared to submit ourselves humbly to His will.

Our human concerns prevent us from focusing our minds on God and thus prevent us from becoming saints. Often when we are faced with a certain situation, our imagination runs wild, thinking of the endless possibilities or outcomes that could occur. We think of all the success and failure, joy, pain, pleasure, and problems that could be involved. But all of these are nothing but a distraction to our sanctity. Only one thing matters to those who want to love God, and that is that we faithfully fulfill the will of God.

"Lord, what is it that you want of me now?" In providing an answer to this question, our faith demolishes all our human concerns, for "all things conspire unto good for those who love God." In making God's will our only goal, Heaven or union with God our only aim, and fidelity our only ambition, we become indifferent to success and failure in this world, and we make our motto, "All for the glory of God."

Loving God is precisely about doing His will; there is no such thing as disobedient love. A soul in love with God wants for nothing but God's will in each moment of the day, realizing that by doing God's will he is slowly turning the tables on the unclean sowers of hatred who think that man is but an animal; thus, he helps to bring about the harmonious and peaceful living that is synonymous with Christ's reign on the earth. But this can only be achieved at some cost to oneself. Indeed, a soul in love is always generous.

Despite our great need, this call to holiness, the call to be a saint, is not one that is new to the twentieth century. Quite the contrary. Sanctity is the will of God for every soul ever created. Nearly two thousand years ago Saint Paul instructed the early Christians in this truth when he wrote, "This is the will of God: that you be saints" (1 Thessalonians 4:3). Indeed, it is the will of God that justifies our very existence.

WE NEED A PLAN

If the wonderful ideal of sanctity, proclaimed for nearly two thousand years among Christians, is to be achieved by you and me individually, then there must be some practical implications.

As we have said, two characteristics of love are consistency and perseverance. If we are to love God by grasping each moment of the day consistently and perseveringly for Him, then our prayer lives must also be consistent. A practical way in which everybody can achieve this is by putting together a pattern or plan of practicing prayer and the sacraments. By then struggling to live this plan day in, day out, we will bring consistency to our relationship with God, and this will be reflected in the words and actions of our lives.

There are many things that we can do to develop and nurture our spiritual lives. The main reasons for these practices, which constitute our interior life, are to show God that we love Him and to develop and feed the soul so that this love can grow. In fact, everything that we do every day can serve as a means of expressing our love for God. However, it is important that at different times throughout the day we give small parcels of time specifically and entirely to God.

Some practices common in the lives of the saints include meditation, regular Mass and confession, the rosary, some time each day in friendly mental dialogue with Jesus as friend, reflection on the Scriptures, the Angelus, and some form of spiritual reading. These give birth to virtue and are the building blocks of the spiritual life. With our life of prayer, we are trying to build a castle within us in which Christ may live. Day by day we place one block on top of another.

Apart from these practices, there are many other devotions and practices of prayer; it is up to each individual to choose as many or as few as he or she wishes. The key is to practice them consistently. Put together a plan and write it down: "I'll do these every day, these every week, and these once a month." Then examine yourself toward the end of each day for one or two minutes: "Did I do my spiritual exercises today? Did I do them well? How can I do them better?" By struggling to move closer to God the next day, we will begin to grow in holiness.

These spiritual exercises, these small parcels of time planted throughout our days, are the telephone poles that hold up the wire of our spiritual life. If the wire hits the ground, we have a problem. If you put too much distance between two telephone poles, the wire will hit the ground. If we do our first spiritual exercise shortly after we wake up in the morning, we must then have firmly in our minds when our next time of prayer during the day is going to be. If we don't, it is almost inevitable that the worries and activities of the world will swallow up the time we have set aside for prayer. We must always have in our minds where the next telephone pole is; otherwise we are going to crash spiritually.

Putting together a pattern or a plan is a practical way of attempting to grow in holiness. The pattern can start from just one daily practice and an examination of conscience and build from there. However, not only must it grow in terms of number of practices and amount of time, it also and more importantly must grow in intensity and depth.

Without a plan we will never develop spiritually.

GOD WANTS EVERYTHING

God wants everything, and in return He will give much more than we could ever imagine. God has a unique plan for each of us that is much greater than any plan that we could put together for ourselves. "No eye has seen, nor ear has heard, nor has it entered into the mind of man, anything as beautiful as what God has prepared for those who love him" (1 Corinthians 2:9).

God is waiting for us to give our lives to Him once and for all, instead of holding back some part of ourselves. So often what we hold back is the very thing that separates us from God and makes us slaves to our senses. We give everything to God by making Christ the center of all our activity. This is only achieved by recognizing Christ's presence throughout the day. By praying we come to know Christ so that we will recognize Him when He crosses our path and will be able to say, "It is the Lord" (John 21:7). In those moments when our hearts burn within us, we will see that Jesus is accompanying us through our lives, making our lives a journey along the road to Emmaus.

EVERYTHING FLOWS FROM OUR LOVE FOR GOD

"All things conspire unto good for those who love God." It is by loving God that we are able to see the things of this world as they really are, because this love allows us to see them in the light of faith. It is only men and women of faith who have true depth and perspective in their lives.

For those who love God, there is only victory, and this victory is for eternity.

"Seek first the kingdom of God and his justice, and all else will be given in addition" (Matthew 6:33). How clearly it strikes me that all the things that so often mean so much to us, all the things of this world, our Lord sums up in two words: "all else." So great is the kingdom of Heaven that the things of this world pale into insignificance.

SAINTS ARE THE ANSWER FOR THESE TIMES

By living a plan of prayer consistently and perseveringly, we will be better disposed to give each moment of our lives to God. This is precisely what determines our holiness, our sanctity. And it is people who firmly commit themselves to this struggle who will assist God in returning the world to be the place He created it to be.

The influences and effects of individuals' words and actions have made the world the place it is today. Throughout the centuries these individuals were no different than you and me; they came from all walks of life, all occupations, were of all ages, all cultures, all nationalities.

God wants to raise up individuals today to be great saints in response to the problems of our world and the questions that plague us; He wants these individuals to relieve the confusion of these times with their clear thinking, gentle obedience, and clean living. You and I are the very individuals He wants to raise up—in the many different parts of the world and in a variety of roles—to inspire and encourage others to become holy as well, all for the salvation of souls and the greater glory of God.

Those who are faithful in small matters will be entrusted with larger ones. The first call for all Christians is to be faithful to their Christian vocation, of which the very essence is one's life of prayer.

The call to holiness is an invitation to live in the presence of God, and it is a call to joy. *Personal holiness is the answer to every problem.*

AN INVITATION

In these pages I have tried to share with you the plan of life that the voice of God has proposed to me over the last four years. I have established that the purpose of each human being is to struggle and grow toward his or her fulfillment. It is this struggle, this growth that brings a person joy. This joy is a foretaste of the union with God that we call Heaven.

For more than four years now, I have engaged in this struggle. It has been the most fulfilling exercise of my life. I have never known such joy and serenity as that which I know when I engage in the struggle.

Just as there are many aspects to our daily lives as human beings, so there are many aspects to this spiritual struggle. I have tried to cover as many as possible in these pages. However, it is not important that we cover every aspect. What is important is that we understand the general principle.

If your goal is to allow the image of God to increase in you by struggling to grow in the likeness of Jesus Christ, then this is the general principle: every moment comes bearing a gift.

Each moment is an opportunity. Every set of circumstances provides you with a chance to learn, to grow, and to love God, yourself, your neighbor, and all of creation. Prayer opens your heart and mind and allows you to see these opportunities. Often they will cost you something. What you receive is always more than what you are asked to give. He that gives lives.

Love is about stepping out of the comfort zone.

Life is meant to be a dance for joy. Be careful how you define joy in your life. The soul hungers for this joy and the journeying soul is always seeking it. The journey is the joy. The joy is the struggle. The struggle is the journey.

Take time to listen occasionally, and remember:

> The journey is the struggle to seek, discover, and live truth.

—⁓—

The joy comes from the struggle.

—⁓⁓—

Remember "the struggle" is the struggle to better yourself, to change, and to grow with courage and patience.

—⁓⁓—

Only two things exist in eternity: joy and misery.

—⁓⁓—

You will not be any happier today than you were yesterday unless you do something different, or at least in a different manner, with a different state of mind or heart.

—⁓⁓—

There are some basic guidelines for making resolutions. Make few of them, preferably one at a time. Write each resolution down. Resolve first to perform your duties and obligations. Examine yourself with regard to your resolution early in the morning and before you retire at night. Do what you resolve. P.S. And when you fail, do not quit. Trust in God, humble yourself, and renew your resolution.

—⁓⁓—

Often it is the ordinary, the everyday, the material that connect us with the spiritual.

—⁓⁓—

Love is truth lived.

—⁓⁓—

Joy is the fruit of appreciation.

—⁓⁓—

Suffering puts us in touch with what is really important. Sacrifice spells out commitment and confirms love.

—⁓—

The Spirit is joy. When we sin, we choose misery and reject joy.

—⁓—

Prayer allows us to see the person we are and the person that we can be.

—⁓—

Truth is the only thing worth living for and the only thing worth dying for.

—⁓—

My obedience to what I know is right brings me joy. My disobedience to what I know is right brings me misery.

—⁓—

Joy is not the absence of pain.

—⁓—

Strength of character comes from prayer.

—⁓—

Your fears are a passport to a new state, to a higher level, to a greater joy.

—⁓—

We become what we love.

—⁓—

What you become is more important than what you do.

This path is a difficult one. It is a path of struggle and heartache, and you will experience both victory and defeat, and defeat upon defeat, but if you persevere you will emerge victorious and fulfilled.

The struggle has a single goal. The tools that help us to maintain the struggle have a single aim. The goal is to live in the presence of God—to recognize that "God is with us, and indeed, within us."

When Mary came to visit Elizabeth, we are told that the child, John the Baptist, *danced for joy* in the womb of Elizabeth. Why? He was in the presence of God.

We also read in the Scriptures that David *danced for joy* before the ark of the covenant. Why? He was in the presence of God.

When we live in the presence of God, our lives become a *dance for joy.*

There is only one goal, there is only one aim, to live in the presence of God. It is what we desire for eternity and indeed for every moment of our existence. This single idea represents everything good that we desire. Peace, joy, love, happiness belong to those who live in the presence of God.

I have shared with you the principles and ideas that the voice of God has shared with me. I offer them to you as they were offered to me, to be accepted and employed or rejected and discarded.

—∿∿—

There once was a very wise old hermit living in a small cave high in the mountains. Late each evening, he would walk for many miles, praying and reflecting on the beauty of creation with which God had surrounded him.

One night when he returned to his cave, he discovered a thief who had come to rob him. The hermit's presence startled the thief, and an uneasy silence filled the cave. After a few moments the wise old man said to the thief, "I have only three things in this world: the bowl from which I eat, and you can have it; the mat on which I sleep, and you can have it; but the third thing I could not possibly give you, so gather the first two and be on your way."

Far from being satisfied, the thief only became curious about the hermit's third possession and said, "What is the third thing you cannot give me?"

The hermit replied, "Follow me," and led the thief out into the night.

They walked through the mountains for miles without exchanging a word until they came to a lake. They stopped on the shore and the hermit stretched his arm out toward the lake and pointed to a beautiful shining silver disk in the middle. The thief stood and stared in silence.

The hermit said quietly and gently, "There is the third thing. It is the face of the moon reflected in the water. It is the wonder and glory of God reflected in His creation. I come here often, and I contemplate the wonder of God and His creation. I recognize the love that God has for His creation. I see that His love for me is great. It is out of this love for me that He has surrounded me with such beautiful, complex, awesome wonders. Yet while they are magnificent and beautiful, glorious and mysterious, I know that they are only a dim reflection of the God who created them—so great is God. It is in recognizing how wide and deep God's love is that I see that the love of God I have experienced in my life is only a portion of the love He has for me. I see the need to open myself a little more to His love."

A silence fell between the two again. The thief knew he could not possibly take this from the wise old man. More than this, the thief was in awe of the fact that there was a man who had something so great, something of greater value than anything he had ever possessed, yet nobody could ever take it from him.

The hermit stretched out his arm toward the disk once again and broke the silence, saying, "I can point you to it, but I cannot give it to you."

Go now and seek it and you will receive abundantly.

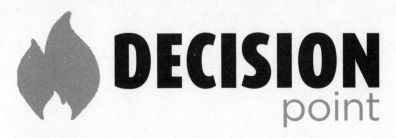

DECISION
point

THE DYNAMIC CATHOLIC
CONFIRMATION EXPERIENCE

"I am convinced this is the best invitation to young Catholics to accept and live their faith that I have encountered."

— CARDINAL DONALD WUERL, Archbishop of Washington

REQUEST YOUR FREE* PROGRAM PACK
at DynamicCatholic.com/Confirmation

The complimentary program pack includes: the complete DVD series containing 72 short films, the student workbook, and the leader guide.

*Just pay shipping.

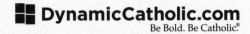

DynamicCatholic.com
Be Bold. Be Catholic.®

NOTES

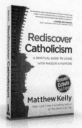

NOTES

NOTES

NOTES

NOTES

NOTES

THE
DYNAMIC CATHOLIC
INSTITUTE

[MISSION]

To re-energize the Catholic Church
in America by developing world-class
resources that inspire people to
rediscover the genius of Catholicism.

[VISION]

To be the innovative leader in the
New Evangelization helping Catholics
and their parishes become
the-best-version-of-themselves.

■■ DynamicCatholic.com
Be Bold. Be Catholic.®

The Dynamic Catholic Institute
2200 Arbor Tech Drive • Hebron, KY 41048
Phone: 1-859-980-7900
Email: info@DynamicCatholic.com